International Crises
and the Role of Law

CYPRUS
1958–1967

THOMAS EHRLICH

CYPRUS
1958–1967

*International Crises
and the Role of Law*

Published under the auspices
of the American Society of International Law

1974

OXFORD UNIVERSITY PRESS

New York and London

FOREWORD

IF we want law and legal institutions to play larger and more effective roles in coping with international conflict, we shall need to understand more clearly the roles they now play. This book is one significant step in the search for such understanding. It is the product of a keen and experienced mind looking closely at one international crisis to learn more about the ways in which law affected—and failed to affect—decisions that were being made.

Under the auspices of the American Society of International Law, a group of us set out, individually and collectively, to learn more about the roles which law plays in the making of decisions at a time of crisis—a crisis which involves issues of war and peace. That legal considerations do play various roles in many important government decisions is clear. It is also clear that many other factors—military, political, economic, psychological, historical, cultural, social, and so forth—also have effect on such decisions. Little is to be gained through argument over the comparative importance in any one decision of the different contributing elements. That law played a ten per cent role or a sixty per cent role tells us nothing about how to increase that role. What one needs to know is not *how much* did law affect a given decision, but *how*. What are the different ways in which law and legal institutions affect what happens in international affairs? This book is part of the quest for useful categories of thought to help us all to understand better how international law works and how it fails to work. It is part of the search for practical insight that may lay a foundation for measures designed to expand or strengthen the roles which law plays.

Work of the American Society of International Law in this sphere was made possible by a generous grant of the Old Dominion Foundation (a predecessor to the Andrew W. Mellon Foundation). This monograph has been commissioned and is published under the auspices of the American Society of International Law. Although the author retains full responsibility for the text, an earlier draft of the text was reviewed and discussed by a panel of members of the Society in furtherance of the project. As chairman of the panel, I would like to express our appreciation to the Foundation, to the Society, and particularly to its Executive Director, Professor Stephen M. Schwebel, for supporting and guiding this project from conception to fruition.

Harvard Law School   ROGER FISHER

PREFACE

THE opportunity to consider international problems concerning Cyprus was first afforded me in 1963-4 by George W. Ball, then Under Secretary of State, when I worked as his special assistant. He taught me much about the sound operations of the legal process in international and domestic affairs—what are and can be the creative roles of law and lawyers in those affairs.

Just before then, my service in the Legal Adviser's Office of the State Department brought me into the closest intellectual relationship with two international lawyers who have been teaching me ever since—Professors Abram Chayes and Andreas F. Lowenfeld. I owe them the profoundest debt. In particular, our collaboration on a set of teaching materials, *International Legal Process*, provided an overall approach to the problems considered here.

This book is part of a project designed and organized by Professor Roger Fisher and guided by a panel of international and legal scholars. Professor Fisher and the other panel members reviewed drafts of the manuscript and gave wise counsel. I am especially appreciative to the three panel members who wrote the comments that appear at the end of the text—Professors Louis Henkin, Edwin C. Hoyt, and Hans A. Linde.

The project was supported by the American Society of International Law. I am most grateful for that support, and for the help of the Society's Executive Director, Stephen M. Schwebel, and its Director of Studies, John Lawrence Hargrove.

Many of my colleagues at Stanford Law School were helpful at various stages of this work. Perhaps most important, they encouraged me to believe that a law dean can and should spend time in scholarly pursuits.

Students at the Stanford Law School in my international law courses over several years aided in developing and testing the ideas presented here. I am especially indebted to Edgar D. Ackerman, Frederick D. Baron, and Gary R. Roberts for their extensive research assistance. Sheila Chilton, Louisa Clemens, Margaret Dickson, and Betsy Reed provided secretarial assistance with uniform good cheer. Jeanne Kennedy worked with great skill in preparing the index.

Finally, before I began writing and in reviewing drafts, I received information and insights from representatives of almost every government and international organization concerned with the island of Cyprus from 1958 to 1967. I did so on the understanding that their names would not be published, but that should not preclude acknowledgement of my gratitude to them.

September 1973   T. E.

CONTENTS

ABBREVIATIONS

Am. J. Int'l L.	American Journal of International Law
Brit. Yb. Int'l L.	British Journal of International Law
Chicago B. Record	Chicago Bar Record
Comnd.	British Command Papers
Cyprus Bull.	Cyprus Bulletin
Dep't of State Bull.	Department of State Bulletin
H.C. Deb.	House of Commons Debates
I.C.J.	International Court of Justice
Int'l & Comp. L.Q.	International and Comparative Law Quarterly
L.N.T.S.	League of Nations Treaty Series
R.S.C.C.	Reports of the Supreme Constitutional Court of Cyprus
Stan. L. Rev.	Stanford Law Review
T.I.A.S.	United States Treaties and Other International Agreements
Transact. Grot. Soc'y	Transactions of the Grotius Society
U. Chi. L. Rev.	University of Chicago Law Review
U.N. Conf. Int'l Org. Docs.	Documents of the United Nations Conference on International Organization (1945)
U.N. Doc.	United Nations Document
U.N. GAOR	United Nations General Assembly Official Records
U.N. SCOR	United Nations Security Council Official Records
U.N. SCPR	United Nations Security Council Provisional Records
U.N.T.S.	United Nations Treaty Series

I

INTRODUCTION*

STATISTICS concerning Cyprus are deceptive. It is hard to believe that a territory so small and with so few people could so disturb the peace of the world. About 600,000 people live on the Island's 3,600 square miles; approximately eighty per cent are of Greek descent; virtually all of the rest are of Turkish extraction. Cyprus has few natural resources; copper is its only significant exportable asset. Lack of water is a perennial problem, and only six per cent of its soil is irrigable. The average annual *per capita* income is 400 dollars, but over half the inhabitants live on farms and subsist on about 300 dollars per year.[1]

Cyprus does have one important asset—its strategic location. It is the third-largest Mediterranean island and is well situated for policing the entire Levant. This asset has made Cyprus a bloody battleground for centuries. It was conquered by Egypt, colonized by Greece, and annexed by Rome before the first century A.D., and for the next two thousand years a succession of absentee landlords ruled its shores. The strength and wisdom of their dominion varied, but not their basic purpose—hegemony over the Eastern Mediterranean by controlling its major island command post. From before the Byzantine era through successive occupations by Richard the Lionheart, the Templars, Franks, Venetians, and Turks, Cyprus was passed with abandon among ruling powers.[2]

The Island's strategic position also led to British acquisition of it in 1878. In exchange for both tribute and British agreement to aid in Turkey's defence against Russia, the Turkish Sultan agreed 'to assign the Island of Cyprus to be occupied and administered

---

* Portions of this introduction and of Chapters III and IV are adapted from Ehrlich, 'Cyprus, the "Warlike Isle": Origins and Elements of the Current Crisis', 18 Stan. L. Rev. 1021 (1965), and from Chayes, Ehrlich, and Lowenfeld, *International Legal Process*, Problem XVI (1969).

[1] See Meyer, *The Economy of Cyprus* 17 (1962).

[2] The definitive chronicle of the Island for 1948 in Hill, *A History of Cyprus* (4 vols., 1949).

by England'.[3] The arrangement was to be terminated and Cyprus restored to Turkey when Turkey regained three Armenian territories from Russia. Until then, Britain would control Cyprus, though titular sovereignty would remain in Turkey. When Turkey allied with Germany at the outset of World War I, Britain renounced the 1878 Agreement and annexed the Island. Though by a 1921 treaty Russia transferred to Turkey two of the three Armenian territories referred to in the 1878 Convention,[4] England retained control over Cyprus. Greece and Turkey acknowledged British sovereignty over the Island by the Treaty of Lausanne in 1923,[5] and in March 1925 the Island was declared a British Crown Colony.

Pressures to end British rule built up slowly until World War II, and rapidly thereafter. Greeks and Greek Cypriots joined in calling for enosis—the Union of Cyprus with Greece. Turkey and the Turkish Cypriots rejected such a step, however, and supported increasingly repressive measures imposed by British authorities on Cyprus to check the agitation of the enosists. Finally, Britain agreed in 1958 to relinquish its rule, not to Greece but to an independent Republic of Cyprus. In 1960 the Island became a sovereign state for the first time in its history. The British grant of independence was, however, tied to a complex series of international agreements.[6] Those Accords—signed by Greece, Turkey, the United Kingdom, and representatives of the Greek and Turkish communities on Cyprus—structured and limited both internal Cypriot affairs and Cypriot relations with other nations.

[3] Convention of Defensive Alliance Between Great Britain and Turkey With Respect to the Asiatic Provinces of Turkey, 4 June 1878, art. I, in 82 *Accounts and Papers* 3–4 (1878).

[4] The treaty, concluded 16 Mar. 1921, is printed in 16 *Martens N.R.G.* (3ᵉ sér) 37.

[5] Treaty of Lausanne, art. 20, 24 July 1923, 28 L.N.T.S. 12, 25 (1924). The British annexation was also acknowledged by Turkey in article 115 of the Treaty of Sèvres, 28 June 1919, in 2 *The Treaties of Peace, 1919–1923*, at 821, 966 (Martin ed., 1924).

[6] Three multinational committees were established to work out final arrangements 'for the transfer of sovereignty in Cyprus'. Conference on Cyprus, Cmnd. 679, at 14 (Document XXX) (1959). The result of their deliberations, which lasted more than a year, is a 220-page document containing the draft treaties, the draft Cypriot constitution, fifteen draft exchanges of notes, and several draft statements. All of the settlement documents are contained in Cyprus, Cmnd. 1093 (1960). The Treaties of Establishment and Guarantee are also contained in Cmnds. 1252, 1253 (Document XXXIV) (T.S. Nos. 4, 5 of 1961) respectively.

They were concluded amid high hopes that they would bring peace as well as independence to a land that had known neither.

Violence erupted on Cyprus three years later, in December 1963. Within days the Island became the centre of a major international crisis. The conduct of world affairs had developed, if not advanced, from the time when the Great Powers of Europe sent a flotilla of gunboats to settle a civil insurrection on Crete. Yet a multilateral force was unquestionably required to keep the peace on Cyprus. After several false starts the United Nations sent such a force and began its effort to resolve—or at least to contain, if not resolve—the crisis. The organization has been engaged in that undertaking ever since.

Much of the period since December 1963 has been marked by the threat of Turkish military intervention to protect the Turkish Cypriot minority. On several occasions, a combination of international pressures was successful in checking the actual use of force by Turkey. But in August 1964, when Greek Cypriot forces attacked several Turkish Cypriot villages, Turkish planes bombed the attackers. In the autumn of 1967, Turkey again threatened to invade the Island, but it held its hand when Greece agreed to withdraw all its soldiers on Cyprus in excess of the contingent authorized under the 1960 settlement.

This study analyses four key decisions concerning Cyprus by four different governments: (1) the British Government's decision in 1958 to relinquish sovereignty over Cyprus; (2) the Cypriot Government's decision in 1963 to propose revisions of the Zurich–London settlement; (3) the Turkish Government's decision in 1964 to bomb the Island; and (4) the Greek Government's decision in 1967 to withdraw its troops from Cyprus. The primary focus of this analysis is the role of legal norms and institutions in each government's decision-making process. Within that framework, the study is particularly concerned with how law was brought to bear by foreign governments and international institutions on national decision-makers. The four decisions were not the only significant ones concerning Cyprus in the 1950s and 1960s, or necessarily the most important in the Island's recent history. Rather, they were chosen because they provide an opportunity, in a single international context, to examine the impact of law on each of four governments—both in its own decisions and in the pressures it brought to bear on decision-making by the others.

Diplomacy, economic and military interests, strong doses of propaganda, and other international forces played important roles in each of the four decisions. These forces interacted with powerful domestic demands. Any study that concentrates on one set of factors in a decision inevitably runs the risk of slanting neutral inquiry, and of appearing to make those factors more significant than they actually were. At the same time, analysis of one set of elements in a decision-making process is not possible unless those elements are singled out for special attention. That is no less true of a legal analysis than of an economic, military, or other examination. This inquiry tries to emphasize legal considerations without being myopic about other forces.

Law is here defined in terms of the probable perceptions of participants in each decision. The term includes norms and institutional arrangements that those involved in the decisions apparently viewed as law and as relevant to the decisions. This approach was adopted as particularly useful in seeking insights into the reach of law into national decisions in international crises. It also seems appropriate to an analysis of the ways in which law can become a more effective means for ordering those affairs.

Some of my judgements about the perceptions of particular participants may, of course, be wrong. I discussed each of the four decisions with representatives of various national governments and international organizations. They reviewed drafts of this study, and I made revisions in light of their comments. But the possibility remains that I am mistaken in concluding that a given issue was perceived as primarily legal. In my view, however, the consequences of such mistakes would generally not be serious in terms of the conclusions drawn from this study. For most of the matters discussed in the study, law presents just one of several interrelated facets. The primary concern is 'how' law affects international decisions rather than 'how much'. The relative impact of legal principles as opposed to other factors is less significant than the variety of roles for law in international affairs. 'Self-determination', for example, is a legal norm embodied in the United Nations Charter and many resolutions of its constituent bodies. But it also expresses a set of moral judgements about fundamental human rights. When Greek representatives to the United Nations called for Cypriot 'self-determination' in the 1950s, it matters less whether they viewed the legal or moral dimensions of the norm as dominant than that those dimensions were closely intertwined and that, like all sound legal standards, this one is rooted in basic moral values.

Law has many dimensions outside the perceptions of actors, and mention of alternative frameworks for analysis may underscore the limitations of this one. One can ask 'What is the law?' concerning a particular issue, either with or without reference to a particular decision-making institution such as the World Court. One can ask 'What should be the law?', again with or without reference to an organization such as the International Law Commission. Further, one can try to step back and consider what difference it would have made if a particular standard or procedure had not been perceived both as law and as relevant in solving a problem. My point is not to examine the relative merits of such alternative approaches but rather to disclaim adoption of any one of them. The paper also makes no claim of contribution to the jurisprudence of international law, though the definition of law used here is obviously inconsistent with the views of some theorists.

Even within the dimensions set off by a perceptual approach, the methodology employed here imposes limitations. The analysis breaks no new methodological ground. Principal reliance was placed on written materials, both primary and secondary. I made no effort to explore every dimension of how the perceptions of law by particular actors affected their actions at particular times. Such an inquiry, and the development of its methodological underpinnings, would require a complex set of tools far beyond the scope of this analysis. It is unlikely, for example, that any individual perceives the full scope of the pressures on him at the time he influences a decision, let alone after the fact. My own inquiries revealed that perceptions of the role of law in a particular decision varied sharply among representatives of the same government.

My concern here is less with how much law affects national decisions than with the ways in which they are affected. Each decision is examined in the total context in which it arose, but the legal framework receives primary attention. The study attempts to lay a basis for judgement on a set of interrelated questions. In what ways does law operate to define and limit the objectives of nations and the optimal means for realizing those objectives? To what extent does the appeal for world support by opposing nations in an international crisis depend on the strength and coherence of their legal positions? In what circumstance does law provide a procedural setting to forge economic, military, and other pressures, and to structure the components of a national decision? How effective is the force of law in establishing and utilizing institutional arrangements for containing and trying to resolve conflicts? Most important, what steps can be taken to improve and strengthen the role of law in ordering relations among nations? Based on the analysis of the four decisions, the final section of this study attempts to draw some conclusions about these and related issues.

II

THE BRITISH GOVERNMENT'S DECISION IN 1958 TO RELINQUISH SOVEREIGNTY OVER CYPRUS

'[T]HERE can be no question of any change of sovereignty in Cyprus,' declared the British Minister of State for Colonial Affairs in 1954.[1] The starting place for any consideration of Cyprus, said the British representative to the United Nations in 1958, is that 'sovereignty of the island is now vested in us'.[2] Sovereignty was more than a starting place for British policy. It was the framework within which British decision-makers considered the Island and its future. In 1958, they decided to abandon that framework. This section focuses on the ways in which legal norms and institutions influenced that decision.

It is not difficult to isolate the main political forces behind maintaining British sovereignty. Strategic considerations, particularly protection of her oil interests, and a deeply rooted desire to retain at least one Mediterranean remnant of the Empire east of Gibraltar were the most important. British officials also claimed an obligation to the Turkish Cypriot minority not to allow the Island to become part of Greece; until 1958, enosis, or union with Greece, was the only seriously considered alternative to British sovereignty. There were other pressures as well, but strategy and pride predominated.

In 1954 the British were forced to withdraw their military bases from Suez. The result was a blow to British military power in the Mediterranean and an even more serious blow to British self-esteem. The forcible ouster of the British Middle East Command Headquarters was a sign, real and symbolic, of England's retreat from the company of great powers. The domestic impact was profound. The Tory Government just managed to quash a back-bench revolt in the House of Commons. In large measure, mutiny was checked by repeated assurances that England would

[1] 531 H.C. Deb. (5th ser.) 507 (1954).
[2] 13 U.N. GAOR 148 (1958).

'never' give up its new Middle Eastern Command Headquarters in Cyprus.[3] Labour members objected. They stressed that Churchill and Roosevelt had called in the Atlantic Charter for the self-determination of all peoples. And why, they asked, should anyone suppose that it would be easier to hold Cyprus than Suez? The Government's stand, charged the Labour Party, was an open invitation to the Cypriot people to escalate the level of violence on the Island until the British would be forced to leave there also. But the 'never' statements calmed the tempers of the Tory backbenchers who saw the Empire sliding into the sea.

During the 1950s, Britain proposed a series of constitutional arrangements to provide 'limited self-government' over the Island's internal affairs. The first of those proposals would have expanded substantially the degree of Cypriot autonomy compared to the existing arrangements; each new plan would have increased the scope of that autonomy even further. But all the schemes assumed maintenance of British sovereignty, at least within the foreseeable future. England rejected the possibility of a new framework in 1954, hinted at it in 1955, recognized it in 1956 as a possible subject of future discussion, and accepted it in 1957 as a matter for an agenda seven years hence. But it was not until late 1958 that the British agreed to abandon the framework itself and to replace it by Cypriot independence with substantial protection for British interests.

It appears likely that the issue was not resolved as a matter of Government policy until December 1958 when the British representative to the United Nations arranged a meeting between the Greek and Turkish Foreign Ministers. Their talks continued through the next month and led to the basic design of the 1960 Accords at a conference in Zurich. For our purposes, the key decision was announced just before that conference when the British Government stated that, provided its 'military requirements were met, in a manner which could not be challenged, by the retention of bases under British sovereignty, together with the provision of the necessary rights and facilities for their operation . . . [it was] prepared to consider the transfer of sovereignty by Her Majesty's Government over the rest of the island'.[4]

---

[3] See, e.g., 531 H.C. Deb. (5th ser.) 507–10 (1954).
[4] 600 H.C. Deb. (5th ser.) 618 (1959).

A. PRESSURES FROM GREEK CYPRIOTS

Greek Cypriots were the principal claimants for a change in the British position. But their institutional means to promote change were limited. The British refused to discuss revision of British sovereignty at meetings with Cypriot leaders; the question was beyond the realm of discussion. No international forum recognized the standing of Greek Cypriots to consider the matter. They were subject people with only limited rights to debate the terms of their subjection, and with no rights to argue the underlying issue.

As early as 1830, substantial sentiment was voiced on the Island for enosis. Pressures built up steadily and unremittently in the next century. The roots of the desire for union cannot be found among the ruins of ancient Greece; Aphrodite's island was never a part of Hellenic Greece. Though Greeks colonized the Island, they regarded the Cypriots as an alien people. The Hellenic ties of Greek Cypriots are rooted in the Byzantine period rather than in classical times. Religion and language were the major pressures unifying Greece and Cyprus—and their centripetal force was substantial. Many Greek Cypriots considered themselves Greeks living on Cyprus, even though their ancestors had lived there for centuries.

At least once during World War I, Great Britain offered to transfer Cyprus to Greece in exchange for Greek support of Serbia.[5] The Greek rejection of this offer, at least in retrospect, may be one of the great tragedies of Cypriot history, for enosis at that time might have eliminated much of the bloodshed of the next half-century.

In 1931, just one hundred years after the first clear cries of enosis were heard from Cyprus, Greek Cypriots burned the Governor's house in large scale demonstrations for union with Greece. A plebiscite among Greek Cypriots in 1949 should have shattered any British illusions about perpetual rule—ninety-six per cent of the eligible voters favoured union with Greece.[6]

---

[5] See Alastos, *Cyprus in History* 339–44 (1955). The offer to Greece has been characterized by supporters of enosis as an acknowledgement of Cyprus's Hellenic ties, id. at 344, but the British are quick to respond that the offer was withdrawn after it was rejected, see, e.g., 9 U.N. GAOR 53 (1954).

[6] Royal Institute of International Affairs, *Cyprus: The Dispute and the Settlement* 11 (1959).

A year later the head of the Greek Orthodox Church in Cyprus died and a new leader, Archbishop Makarios III, was elected. Only thirty-seven years old at the time of his election, the Archbishop's magnetic manner and style quickly made him the leader of the Greek Cypriot people in secular as well as spiritual affairs.

The Archbishop campaigned for enosis from his pulpit in direct violation of British sedition laws. For six years the British Governor did nothing, fearing that prosecution would trigger an explosion. Priest-politicians were an accepted feature of Cypriot life, but none had the charisma—in its true sense—of Archbishop Makarios. Others were 'ethnarchs', or leaders of their people; the Archbishop united religious fervour, an extraordinary political sense, and a passionate appeal for union with Greece. Some analysts of the Cypriot scene have suggested that his political ambitions extended beyond the Island and that he favoured enosis only as a step to becoming prime minister of the new union. Eleutherios Venizelos, a Cretan, became prime minister of Greece after his successful campaign for the union of Crete with Greece. Archbishop Makarios may have hoped to follow that path, although he publicly denied such ambitions.[7] Perhaps the only certain facts are that from the outset of his rule he held the loyalty of the Greek Cypriots and was committed to ending British rule.

It may be that enosis was the Archbishop's goal at the outset, and that after 1958 he pressed for an independent Cyprus only because he feared the British threat of 'double enosis': if some of the Island were to become Greek territory, then part would become Turkish. Or it may be that his call for enosis was designed to force Greece, his only unquestioned sovereign ally, to lead the

---

[7] See Wall, 'Cyprus Problem=Makarios Problem', *N.Y. Times*, 18 Oct. 1964, §6 (Magazine), pp. 38, 110.

One of the United Nations mediators in the Cyprus crisis, Mr. Galo Plaza Lasso, apparently spent some time discussing the question of enosis with the Archbishop, but Mr. Galo Plaza's report is unclear concerning the Archbishop's views on the matter. See U.N. Doc. No. S/6253, at 53–4 (1965). See also Foley, *Legacy of Strife: Cyprus From Rebellion To Civil War* 27 (1964). A collection of 'policy statements' by the Archbishop was published by the Turkish Tourism and Tourist Office, New York City, to prove that 'all his efforts have been directed towards the materialization of Enosis, [although] he sought to create the false impression that he is in favour of an independent State of Cyrpus separate from Greece'. Foreword to *Cyprus: Greek Expansionism or Independence* I (1965).

international campaign for Cypriot freedom from British control. Greek leadership of that campaign was essential because Makarios had no platform beyond the Island from which to press his case; from 1956 to 1958 the British did not even allow him to live on Cyprus but exiled him to the Seychelles Islands.

Greece was certain to exert strong efforts for enosis. No Greek leader in power could afford the domestic pressures that would result from compromise on that issue. Every opposition leader in Greece could be counted on to claim that the Greek Government's efforts had been insufficient. Even in the late 1950s, when many Greek politicians no doubt wished that Cyprus would sink beneath the sea, their strident demands continued on behalf of the Island.

Greek Cypriots designed a two-pronged attack against the British. Within the Island they sought to raise the cost of continued British rule over a hostile population; internationally, they prodded the Greek Government to press for Cypriot self-determination. The two strands were closely related: The more difficulties the British had in maintaining their authority, the more persuasive became Greek arguments that Cypriots wanted self-determination.

The main weapon in the first line of attack was EOKA, a Greek Cypriot terrorist organization. EOKA was organized in 1953 by General George Grivas, a former career officer in the Greek Army who was born and raised in Cyprus. The charter of EOKA declared that the organization was dedicated to focusing 'international public opinion' on the problem of Cyprus 'until international diplomacy—the United Nations—and the British' were forced to solve it.[8] Whatever the uncertainties about the Archbishop's views on enosis, the position of EOKA was clear: union with Greece was the Cypriot manifest destiny. Grivas first returned to the Island after World War II in 1951 under the *nom de guerre* of Dighenis, a legendary Greek hero; within a year he had begun developing plans for an expanding guerrilla campaign. The violent tactics of EOKA, the violent British response, and the bloodshed that resulted from the clash have all been graphically described elsewhere. A Greek Cypriot

---

[8] Grivas-Dighenis, G. *Memoirs of the EOKA Struggle, 1955–1959*, at Appendix, p. 3 (1961) (in Greek). Quoted in Xydis, 'The UN General Assembly as an Instrument of Greek Policy: Cyprus, 1954–58', XII J. of Conflict Resolution 141, 144 (1968).

friend of Lawrence Durrell characterized the situation in terms equally applicable to more recent problems:

First there was no Cyprus problem. Then a few bangs followed and you agreed there was a problem, but it couldn't be solved ever. More bangs followed. Then you agreed to try and solve it, but in fact only to bedevil it further. Meanwhile however EOKA has seen that a few bombs could change your inflexible 'Never' to 'Sometime'; now they feel they have a right to provoke an answer to the question 'When?'[9]

As Aneurin Bevan said in a 1954 debate on the 'never' policy, 'This is an open invitation by the British House of Commons to the people of Cyprus to take whatever measures they think they can take to make things as uncomfortable as possible for us when we establish a base there.'[10]

Archbishop Makarios reportedly had 'grave doubts' about armed action, but by 1954 he gave EOKA at least tacit support.[11] At the outset, the Greek Government gave no official encouragement to Grivas. By 1954, however, its position had also changed to approval of the efforts by Grivas to organize an armed revolt on the Island. In large measure, both shifts were accelerated if not triggered by the British intransigence on the future of Cyprus.

In November 1952, Field-Marshal Papagos and his Greek Rally party won an overwhelming victory in the Greek national election. He had previously promised Archbishop Makarios that he would actively press the British Government to discuss enosis. But Greek efforts to pursue the matter were consistently rebuffed on the ground that Cyprus was a matter of Britain's internal affairs. The issue came to a head in the autumn of 1953 when Anthony Eden told Mr. Papagos that the United Kingdom would 'never' give up Cyprus. Mr. Papagos was furious: 'He told me *never*—not even *we shall see*.'[12]

B. PRESSURES FROM GREECE

Greece made her primary case for enosis in the United Nations General Assembly—the public forum where it would have maximum impact on British policy makers. Greece wrapped that

---

[9] Durrell, *Bitter Lemons* 223–4 (Dutton paperback ed., New York, 1957).
[10] 531 H.C. Deb. (5th ser.) 566 (1954).
[11] Stephens, *Cyprus: A Place of Arms* 134 (1966); Grivas, *The Memoirs of General Grivas* 17–18 (Foley ed., 1964).
[12] Stephens, *Cyprus: A Place of Arms* 135 (1966).

case in the mantle of national self-determination—the legal
norm with widest appeal to General Assembly members. This concept played an important role in shaping Greek objectives, just
as the concept of sovereignty affected both the vision of British
officials and their judgement on what policies best served British
interests.

The General Assembly was seen by Greek representatives as
'the instrument *par excellence* by which world public opinion can
express itself and exert pressures—strong or weak, according to
circumstances—upon international policies'.[13] In 1955, a year
after Greece first took the Cyprus issue to the General Assembly,
there were 75 Assembly members, 25 more than when the
organization was created eight years previously. Many were
former colonies that could be counted on to side with Cyprus on
an issue that went to the roots of their existence. Further, the
number of such supporters could be expected to grow each year.
Since each Assembly member has one vote, there was maximum
opportunity for exposing the Cypriots' plight. The General
Assembly had an additional advantage as a forum for considering
the issue of Cyprus. Greece maintained that once the United
Nations was seized of the matter, no solution could properly be
concluded outside the organization. This was the main Greek
defence against both NATO efforts to settle the problem within
that agency and British attempts to resolve it through tripartite
talks with Turkey and Greece.

The Greek call for Cypriot self-determination was first voiced
in the United Nations in 1954. With more passion than accuracy,
the Greek prime minister wrote to the United Nations Secretary-
General that 'Greece alone has been the lasting element, the
unalterable factor, the only permanent reality in the island of
Cyprus. It would not be enough to repeat that Cyprus belongs to
the Greek world; Cyprus is Greece itself.'[14] Basing Greece's
request upon 'the past, present and future of the Hellenic
nations,' he urged that 'the principle of equal rights and self
determination of peoples,' as expressed in Article 1(2) of the

---

[13] 12 U.N. GAOR 165 (1957). For an exhaustive analysis of Greek efforts
in the General Assembly, see Xydis, *Cyprus, Conflict and Conciliation, 1954–1958*
(1967). For a more concise account, see Xydis, 'The UN General Assembly as an
Instrument of Greek policy: Cyprus, 1954–58', XII J. of Conflict Resolution
141 (1968).
[14] U.N. Doc. A/2703, at 2 (1954).

United Nations Charter, be applied to Cyprus. By this he meant a vote of the Cypriot people, under United Nations auspices, to decide their future. In light of the 1949 plebiscite, there could have been little doubt about the outcome of such a vote.

Greece based her case for United Nations jurisdiction on three Charter articles.[15] First, she claimed that Cypriots had been denied the application of 'the principle of equal rights and self-determination', under Article 1(2). She maintained that the United Kingdom had a contractual obligation to respect that principle, an obligation that had been affirmed by two General Assembly resolutions.[16] Second, Greece argued that the General Assembly was authorized under Article 10 to discuss any question or matter arising under the Charter, including the right to self-determination as expressed in Article 1(12). Finally, Greece referred to the General Assembly's authority under Article 14 to 'recommend measures for the peaceful adjustment of any situation, including situations resulting from a violation of the provisions of the Charter setting forth the purposes and principles of the United Nations'. Greece claimed that the United Kingdom had violated those principles by denying Cypriots the right to determine their own future.

Although Greece succeeded in including the issue on the agenda, the General Assembly declared that 'for the time being, it does not appear appropriate to adopt a resolution on the question of Cyprus . . .'[17] But Greek representatives declared that they had won an important tactical victory: Cyprus was no longer an internal matter of British policy; it was an international question.[18] For the next four years Greece tried to obtain a

---

[15] 9 U.N. GAOR, Gen. Comm. 7–11 (1954).

[16] G.A. Res. 545, 6 U.N. GAOR 375, U.N. Doc. A/L.102 (1952); G.A. Res. 637, 7 U.N. GAOR 367, U.N. Doc. A/Resolution/40 (1952).

[17] 9 U.N. GAOR Supp. 21, at 5, U.N. Doc. A/2890 (1954).

[18] Both the British and the Greek representatives claimed success. 'I believe that the vote which has just taken place,' said Mr. Nutting, the British representative, 'represents a great and imporant victory for common sense. It shows how much support there is in this Assembly for the view put forward by the United Kingdom from the outset that, legal considerations altogether apart, a full-dress discussion on Cyprus could achieve no useful purpose.' The Greek representative, Mr. Kyron, responded: 'The affirmative vote of the representative of the United Kingdom is a formal recognition on the part of his Government of the fact that what the United Kingdom Government has persistently called a domestic issue, and one closed forever, has now become a wide-open international problem.' 9 U.N. GAOR 539–40 (1954).

General Assembly recommendation in support of her position. Each year it failed. Nevertheless, the pressures of defending the British position took a substantial toll on its representatives and their ability to maintain Britain's prestige in the world organization.

For the most part, the Greek arguments to the General Assembly from 1955 through 1958 followed the pattern of 1954: the United Nations Charter guaranteed to the Cypriot people the right of self-determination, and England was violating that right by maintaining sovereignty over Cyprus. But there were new elements introduced in each debate. In 1956, for example, a Greek draft resolution called for a seven-nation fact-finding committee to investigate both British charges of Greek support for EOKA in violation of international law and Greek charges that British atrocities on the Island violated the fundamental Charter rights of Cypriots.[19]

At the eleventh General Assembly in 1957, a resolution on the Cyprus issue was finally adopted. It was sponsored by India and merely expressed the hope that a 'peaceful, democratic and just solution will be found in accordance with the principles and purposes of the Charter', and urged negotiations toward that end.[20] Although Greece had urged a much stronger resolution, its representatives used this one to good advantage. It provided at least arguable legitimacy for the Greek Government rejection of two proposals to negotiate outside the United Nations. In 1957, the Secretary-General of NATO offered to use his good offices to resolve differences between the British, Greek, and Turkish Governments. The Greek Government feared that the pressures within NATO to force a settlement would inevitably lead to maintenance of British control, for Greece had no newly independent allies in NATO. To most of the NATO members, the

[19] 11 U.N. GAOR, Annexes, Agenda item 55, at 16 (1956).

[20] G.A. Res. 1013, 11 U.N. GAOR 1199 (1956–7). The Greek Government's use of the resolution, summarized here, is described in Xydis, 'The UN General Assembly as an Instrument of Greek Policy: Cyprus, 1954–58', 141, 148. In the twelfth General Assembly session, the Greek Government finally succeeded in persuading a voting majority in the General Assembly to accept a resolution expressing the 'earnest hope that further negotiations and discussions would be undertaken in a spirit of co-operation with a view to having the right of self-determination applied in the case of the people of Cyprus'. U.N. Doc. A/3794, at 2 (1957). But the resolution failed to gain the two-thirds vote necessary to make it a General Assembly 'recommendation with respect to maintenance of international peace and security' under Article 18(2) of the Charter.

issue was an irritant that weakened the organization as a whole. The Greek Government stated publicly, therefore, that it could not bypass the United Nations as long as the issue was pending in that body. Similarly, the Greek Government refused to accept a British offer to convene a new tripartite conference in August 1957, and cited the General Assembly resolution as authority for resolving the matter in direct negotiations between England and the Cypriot people.

Bilateral discussions between British and Cypriots were the apparent goal of the Greek Government. It was increasingly uncomfortable in the role of middleman in a dispute from which it had little chance to benefit, but in which it would be politically involved until a settlement was concluded. Greek leaders presumably still believed that Cyprus *ought* to be part of Greece, that enosis was the just solution. The historical and cultural ties that bound Greeks and Greek Cypriots in the 1940s were no less strong a decade later. But the likelihood of union must have seemed increasingly remote and the political cost internationally of continued pressure for enosis increasingly high.

Archbishop Makarios shifted his negotiating position in 1958, and Greece followed suit. Up to that point, enosis had been the announced goal of the Archbishop; self-determination was a persuasive slogan in pressing the case, but no one seriously disputed the British charge that enosis was his aim. In 1958, however, the Archbishop let it be known that he would accept an independent Cyprus, with appropriate guarantees for the Turkish Cypriot minority.[21] The Greek Government took up the new banner and in the thirteenth General Assembly session introduced a resolution that urged the British Government to help Cyprus move to 'the status of independence'.[22] The resolution was rejected, but the scheme that would end British sovereignty had at last been articulated by one of the principal parties.

Just as Greece turned to the United Nations for support against the British policy of perpetual sovereignty, it also turned to the Commission established by the European Convention on Human

[21] Archbishop Makarios revealed his new scheme in an interview with Mrs. Barbara Castle, Vice-Chairman of the Labour Party. See Foley, *Legacy of Strife* 137–8 (1964).

[22] 13 U.N. GAOR, Annexes, Agenda item 68, at 16 (1958). The Greek Government's arguments for independence were elaborated in various statements by its officials. See 13 U.N. GAOR, 1st Comm. 249, 261 (1958); 13 U.N. GAOR 313 (1958).

Rights for support against the British policy of repressing opposition within the Island. In 1953, the United Kingdom had extended the Convention's coverage to Cyprus. When the British Government imposed emergency measures in 1955, it acknowledged that some were in derogation of its obligations, but contended that such measures were authorized under section 15(1) to meet a 'public emergency threatening the life of the nation . . .'[23]

Greece applied to the Commission established under the Convention, claiming that the conditions required by section 15 had not been met and further that emergency measures allowing whipping and other punishments violated section 3, which is excluded from the exception under section 15. Greece brought its application under section 24, which allows any member to apply to the Commission for a finding that another member has violated the Convention. No special standing is required, and the Convention includes no 'domestic jurisdiction' exception comparable to Article 2(7) of the United Nations Charter. An applicant must make a prima facie showing that the Convention has been violated, but upon that showing the Commission acts *ex officio*. It may look beyond the arguments and evidence presented by the parties, and may not terminate a case until it is satisfied that the Convention has not been breached.

This procedure became a powerful instrument of Greek policy. In June 1956 the Greek application was accepted, thus making the Commission a Greek ally in determining the extent of British repression. The United Kingdom was placed on the defensive, and the very fact of an investigation created a public cloud over British practices in Cyprus. The Commision's sessions and those of an investigating subcommittee were secret, but this policy was two-edged: it restricted the Greek Government's ability to publicize evidence revealed to the Commission; it also provided opportunities to spread rumours about that evidence.

[23] The two Greek applications to the European Commission on Human Rights are described in 2 Yearbook of the European Convention on Human Rights 174–99 (1960); Robertson, *The Law of International Institutions in Europe* 74–5 (1961). The Convention and related documents are in Yearbook of the European Convention on Human Rights, *Documents and Decisions: 1955–1956–1957* (1959).

C. PRESSURES FROM TURKEY AND TURKISH CYPRIOTS

Turkey's interests in Cyprus were based on both the lives of Turkish Cypriots—eighteen per cent of the Island's population—and on the strategic location of Cyprus, close to the Turkish coast. Just as most Greek Cypriots consider themselves Greeks living on Cyprus, even though their ancestors lived on the Island for centuries, most Turkish Cypriots view Turkey as their fatherland, though they have no desire to emigrate. The domestic political pressures within Turkey to protect this minority were as strong as the domestic pressures within Greece. And once the Turkish Government resolved to provide that protection, Turkey was a necessary party to any settlement. To the British, Turkey was a far more important NATO ally than Greece. Not only was Turkey stronger militarily, it was also a buffer between Middle Eastern oil and the Soviet Union. Further, the Baghdad Pact was central to England's plans for promoting British intersts in the area; Turkey was the linchpin of the pact. As Eden wrote in his memoirs, 'I regarded our alliance with Turkey as the first consideration in our policy in that part of the world.'[24]

The Turks borrowed a Churchillian phrase in saying that Cyprus faces their 'soft underbelly'. Only forty miles from Turkey, the Island has been called 'the cork in the bottle of Iskenderun'. As long as the United Kingdom controlled the Island, the Turks had little concern that Cyprus might be used as a staging point for an attack against her territory. But Greece already controlled islands that, together with Cyprus, ringed Turkey's southern ports. Turks still recalled their bitter conflicts with Greece in the early 1920s, and were firmly opposed to enosis.

Turkey was content to let the British take the lead in reponse to both the Greek application to the United Nations in 1954 and the onset of EOKA activities in 1955. England was committed to maintaining the *status quo*, and that was precisely what Turkey and the Turkish Cypriots wanted. Turkey generally seconded the British arguments in the General Assembly, adding only that if Britain were ever to renounce her rights under the Treaty of Lausanne, then Cyprus must revert to Turkey from which those rights were derived.

After 1956, however, Turkey began to assume a more active role in the General Assembly debates. In part, this was because

[24] Eden, *Full Circle* 414 (1960).

the Turkish Cypriots had become more involved in the growing conflict on the Island. They formed the bulk of the expanding police forces, and the first communal fighting broke out when EOKA terrorists killed a Turkish policeman. A Turkish Cypriot organization, VOLKAN, was subsequently formed to combat EOKA. Further, anti-Greek riots in Turkey became increasingly common. These and other forces led the Turkish Government to take the lead on one important issue in the General Assembly debates on Cyprus. As we have seen, self-determination for the Cypriot people was the basic Greek demand. From the ninth to the eleventh Assembly sessions, the Turkish representatives generally responded that the principle of self-determination in Article 1(2) of the Charter could not be used to undermine treaty arrangements concluded by consenting sovereign states; the reference to 'respect for the obligations arising from treaties' in the preamble to the Charter was intended to foreclose precisely the arguments made by Greece concerning the Treaty of Lausanne.[25] But in the twelfth and thirteenth Assembly sessions, the Turkish representative pressed a quite different response to the Greek call for self-determination: if self-determination were allowed, it must be granted to *both* the Greek Cypriot majority *and* the Turkish Cypriot minority.[26] The idea of partition had first been suggested by the British Colonial Secretary in 1956, when he announced the Radcliffe proposals to the House of Commons.[27] The British United Nations representative suggested the plan again in the eleventh Assembly session.[28] It apparently took some time for the argument to take hold in Turkish minds. But when it did, the Turkish Government adopted it wholesale. Cyprus was made up of two distinct peoples, the Turkish delegate to the United Nations claimed, and if the *status quo* were to be altered, each group on the Island should have the right to determine its future. As we will see, the argument ultimately undercut not only the Greek argument for enosis through self-determination, but also much of the strength of the legal case for continued British sovereignty.

[25] See, e.g., 10 U.N. GAOR 55 (1955); 9 U.N. GAOR, 1st Comm. 549–52 (1954).

[26] See, e.g., 12 U.N. GAOR, 1st Comm. 371 (1957).

[27] See 562 H.C. Deb. (5th ser.) 1267–9 (1956).

[28] 11 U.N. GAOR, 1st Comm. 225–6 (1956).

D. THE BRITISH DECISION

The British decision in 1958 is cast here as a judgement to renounce sovereignty over Cyprus. As in all major questions of public policy, the framing of the issue inevitably imposes a special perspective on its resolution. Here one could state the question in other ways: whether base areas on the Island would adequately serve British military needs; whether the increasing costs of terrorist activities were worth the candle; and so forth. But for purposes of analysing the impact of legal norms and institutions on the processes of British decision-making that led to Cypriot independence, the initial characterization seems fair.

The main military, political, and other considerations that led to the decision are discernible, although weighing their relative impact is much more difficult. First, the continuing cost of controlling the Island was high and growing higher. Almost 30,000 British troops were required to check a few hundred EOKA terrorists; there was no end of the violence in sight. As a result of the bloodshed, the entire Greek Cypriot population was rapidly becoming alienated from England; much of the rest of the world viewed the problem with increasing alarm. Second, the British military had concluded, apparently reluctantly, that British strategic needs could be met by maintaining sovereignty over base areas on the Island. This judgement was in turn affected by the revised British military requirements in the wake of the Suez crisis and the Iraqi revolution as well as the military costs of maintaining the Island as an armed camp. Third, Britain was under great pressure from the United States and its NATO allies to resolve a dispute that endangered Greek–Turkish relationships and NATO itself. Fourth, as the numbers of newly independent nations increased throughout the 1950s, so did the intensity of their cries against continued colonialism. Other factors, less significant in themselves, added to the pressures. And all of these forces were intensified by the stand of the British Labour Party that 'the people of Cyprus, like all other peoples, have a right to determine their own future'. [29] This analysis will not focus on these pressures themselves, but rather on the ways in which law may have structured them and their effect on British decision-makers.

[29] British Labour Party, Press Release, 27 Nov. 1957, quoted in Royal Institute of International Affairs, *Cyprus: The Dispute and the Settlement* 39 (1959).

Throughout the 1950s, the British defence of continued control over the Island could be summarized in two principles of international law: the sanctity of treaties and the absolute authority inherent in the concept of sovereignty. The British case could be phrased in the following terms. The Treaty of Lausanne recognized England's sovereignty in Cyprus. The treaty could not be revised without England's consent and nothing could force the granting of that consent: *pacta sunt servanda*. The official British stand on the sanctity of the Lausanne Treaty reflected the arid judgement of Lord McNair: 'As a question of law, there is not much to be said upon the revision of treaties.'[30] The Lausanne Treaty was a solemn international agreement. The idea that law could impose any obligation on England to revise that agreement was a contradiction of terms. Stability and change in this matter were inherently inconsistent.

The British view of sovereignty appeared no less firm. Until and unless England decided otherwise, her right to govern Cyprus could not be questioned—that was what sovereignty was all about. Anthony Eden's memoirs on this point are reminiscent of a nineteenth-century international law text in which sovereignty is considered in terms comparable to a state of grace.[31] One can quibble about the implications of sovereignty and its application to particular problems—especially the appropriate degree of local autonomy—but it is quite unthinkable to question the concept itself. The parallel is overdrawn. But the importance of the norm as a basis for British policy cannot be overstated.

Phrased in terms of maintaining treaty obligations and the rights of sovereignty, England's position appeared to British policy-makers as unassailable under traditional international law. And the fact that the decision did not occur until 1959 can be ascribed, at least in part, to British conceptions of the issue in those terms. Fundamental precepts of international law legitimized the *status quo*.

The problem was compounded in England's relations with Cypriots. International law not only failed to impose an effective obligation on the British to negotiate with Cypriots, it also provided no forum for such negotiations.[32] Cypriots were the group

---

[30] McNair, *The Law of Treaties* 534 (1961).
[31] Eden, *Full Circle* 403 (1960).
[32] Article 73 of the United Nations Charter requires member-states that administer non-self-governing territories 'to promote to the utmost . . . the

most directly affected by British actions on the Island. Yet the
very principles of international law that conferred the status of
absolute authority on England seemed to preclude Cypriots from
any standing to challenge that authority within the international
legal system. No other international body, including the United
Nations, offered colonial peoples a hearing as a matter of right.
These failings contributed both to the time required to resolve
the matter and to the bloodshed that occurred before it was concluded. As we have seen, Greek Cypriots turned to violence when
the British refused to discuss the future status of the Island with
them. A Greek Cypriot friend of Lawrence Durrell put the matter
sharply.

Why were you not honest in the beginning? If you had said, 'This is a
Greek island but we are determined to stay in it and will fight for it,'
do you think a single weapon would have been raised against you?
Never! We know your legal title to the island is unquestionable. But
that small lie is the seed from which all these monstrous things have grown
and will continue to grow.[33]

The Greek Cypriot strategy was to raise the cost of continued
British rule by escalating the level of violence on the Island. This
strategy provided support for Greek arguments in the United
Nations that Cyprus was being retained as a colony against the
will of her people. Equally important, the Island's utility as a
military base was reduced to the extent that British troops stationed there were occupied with Greek Cypriot insurgents.

In part, the British response was military—to take every feas-
ible measure to crush the EOKA movement. When a 1955 Conference in London failed to reach agreement on the terms of
Cypriot self-government, Eden, the British prime minister,
appointed John Harding, the former Chief of the Imperial
General Staff, as Governor. Harding immediately took several
steps toward transforming the Island into an armed camp: a
declaration of a state of emergency; detentions and deportations
without trial; imposition of the death penalty for possessing arms;
mass arrests; and the deportation of Archbishop Makarios.

---

well-being of the inhabitants' of those territories, and that obligation is defined
as including the development of self-government. But neither Article 73 nor any
other Charter provision specifically required England to negotiate the terms
of self-government, let alone independence, with the Cypriot people.

[33] Durrell, *Bitter Lemons* 241–2 (Dutton paperback, New York, 1957).

The British also responded to the Greek Cypriots with a series
of plans that would have revised the structure of government on
the Island to expand the scope of local autonomy. These plans, it
was hoped, would both weaken the unity of Greek Cypriots support for EOKA and diffuse the international pressures. Further,
such proposals would foreclose a Greek challenge that Britain
had failed to fulfil her obligations concerning administration of
non-self-governing territories under Article 73 of the United
Nations Charter. But as each of these schemes was announced,
England's insistence on sovereignty rang increasingly hollow.
Why continue British sovereignty without British rule? In this
sense, therefore, the domestic legal arrangements proposed for
Cyprus undercut England's position in international law. But the
existence of this slow process of erosion should not obscure the
failings of international law to provide effective instruments for
regularizing the process of change in a politically unstable
situation.

In spite of those failings, international law did play an important part in the ultimate British decision to renounce her
sovereignty. It is not possible to quantify the extent to which law
influenced the decision, but the means of that influence can be de-
lineated. For purposes of analysis, those means can be considered
in terms of the three international organizations that debated
the Cyprus situation: The United Nations General Assembly,
the European Commission on Human Rights, and the North
Atlantic Treaty Organization.

(1) *The United Nations General Assembly.* The British were put on
the defensive by the application of the Greek Government to
inscribe the Cyprus question on the General Assembly agenda.
And the slow shifts in the British arguments before that body re-
veal that the Greek offensive may have had a substantial impact
on British officials. In the initial General Assembly debates, the
United Kingdom placed primary emphasis on Article 2(7) of the
Charter: to allow the Greek Application would be an intervention essentially within England's domestic jurisdiction. 'Any
infringement by the United Nations of that fundamental principle would be regarded by the United Kingdom as *ultra vires* and
completely unacceptable.'[34] But the argument that an issue is not

---

[34] 11 U.N. GAOR, 1st Comm. 221 (1957). The United Kingdom also supported a similar argument made by France with regard to Algeria. See 10
U.N. GAOR 174–5 (1956).

a matter of international concern is difficult to maintain in an
international body. The very fact that the problem has been
raised in that forum lends weight to the contention that it is more
than a matter of one nation's domestic policy. The British position was particularly difficult because no more than Assembly
debate was at issue; there is respectable authority for the position
that discussion does not constitute 'intervention' without regard
to the nature of the question being discussed. And the longer the
debate on whether an item is debatable, the more persuasive becomes the affirmative position. All these factors worked in favour
of Greece. By the eleventh General Assembly session, Britain gave
in—the first important wedge was driven in the previously im-
pregnable British case.

The United Kingdom's new line of legal defence was in one
sense a complete reversal of the Article 2(7) contention. The
Cyprus problem was indeed an international issue that could be
discussed in the General Assembly. But it was not simply a
colonial question that could be resolved by negotiations between
British and Cypriots. Rather, it was a complex matter that involved Greece and Turkey as well as the United Kingdom:

Three nations are concerned with the problem of Cyprus. First, the
United Kingdom: the sovereignty of the island is now vested in us.
It is our responsibility to safeguard the peace and well-being of the
Cypriots.

. . . A large majority of the population are Greek Cypriots. In addition to their cultural and religious leanings toward Greece, they aspire
toward union with Greece. Therefore, Greece has a strong interest in the
island. Then there is Turkey. A considerable number of Turkish Cypriots
live in the island, people who look to Turkey as their fatherland. The
island is of great strategic importance to Turkey, covering its southern
ports and has a long association with Turkey in the past.

It is a case, therefore—and this really cannot be disputed—of three
countries having an interest in the problem. It is a tripartite problem.[35]

In the early United Nations debates on Cyprus, the Greek
Government had sought to exclude Turkey from any international negotiations on the Island's future. It claimed that self-
determination was an established principle that the British could
easily apply to Cyprus under procedures negotiated with Greece
and the Cypriots, with enosis as one of the options. The new
position of Britain was the basis for its response to Greece that

[35] 13 U.N. GAOR 148 (1958).

the future of Cyprus posed a complex international problem to which no simple slogan such as self-determination provided a solution.

In an effort to regain the offensive, Greece also revised its stand, contending that 'the United Kingdom representative had been expressing a colonialist point of view in stating that the three Governments referred to were among the parties directly concerned in the Cyprus question. The people of Cyprus constituted the only party directly concerned; the Greek Government, for its part, was merely acting as a spokesman for the Cypriots.' [36] In short, Greece argued that Cyprus was not an international but an internal problem.

The British argument may have been a fine job of lawyering, but it also may have given pause to British decision-makers about the merits of their underlying position. Inconsistent arguments have their place in the criminal courtroom, but their inconsistency is bound to raise questions about the defendant's conduct. When the forum is an international body of nation-states, the problem is accentuated.

The British case based on the Lausanne Treaty stood up better over time, in part because Greece sought to use the treaty in inconsistent ways. On the one hand, Greek representatives argued that Turkey had renounced all its rights and interests in Cyprus by the agreement. On the other hand, they claimed that as to Britain, the treaty could not freeze the *status quo* to deny a colonial people the right of self-determination. In response, Britain maintained that the treaty settled the question of sovereignty over the Island until and unless Britain decided otherwise. Greece and Turkey were both signatories to the treaty; neither had reserved any rights in regard to Cyprus, as Greece had done regarding the Dodecanese Islands. To allow the Greek petition would open up every territorial and boundary agreement. 'If this principle is accepted, then no frontier would be permanent. The way would be open to foment discord, to agitate for territorial adjustments, to cause racial and religious discord, and to use this Organization for these purposes.' [37]

This spectre was enough to discredit the Greek claim in the eyes of many Assembly members. But the argument that a consensual agreement estops the signatories from objecting to its terms does

[36] 13 U.N. GAOR, 1st Comm. 315 (1958).
[37] 9 U.N. GAOR 53 (1954).

not run to the peoples subject to that agreement who had no voice in negotiating its terms. Although this weakness was obscured because the Cypriots had no standing to raise the matter in the Assembly, the point was presumably not lost on British officials. As each British colony gained freedom, the impermanence of colonial domination—and the treaty structure providing its legal base—must have been underscored. The situation of Cyprus raised special problems that slowed the process. But viewing the dismemberment of the Empire over time, the process must have seemed inexorable.

Finally, the Greek demand for Cypriot self-determination ultimately appears to have had a profound impact on the British decision to renounce its sovereignty. At the first two General Assembly sessions that considered Cyprus, United Kingdom representatives rested their position primarily on Article 2(7). Their main substantive response to the demand for self-determination was to charge that the Greek petition was part of a veiled campaign for enosis, and therefore an effort 'to interfere in the domestic affairs of a foreign Power in order to make territorial gains'.[38] But in 1957, as British representatives relaxed their Article 2(7) objection, they also agreed that the principle of self-determination was 'a guide for [Britain's] policy toward its Non-Self-Governing Territories', including Cyprus.[39] Their speeches, however, were filled with ambiguous qualifiers: 'The application of self-determination without any regard to circumstances would be subversive of established government everywhere and could only lead to chaos.'[40]

In December 1956, British officials took a new tack.[41] They announced another set of proposals for 'limited self-government', and said that Greek Cypriots would be given a chance to choose union with Greece if the proposals worked well over a period of time. In the event of Greek Cypriots opting for enosis, however, the Turkish Cypriots would also be allowed a separate vote. And if they chose to join Turkey, the Island would be divided. Although the scheme was never spelled out in detail, presumably Turkey would have received approximately eighteen per cent of the Island, or a piece roughly proportionate to the size of the

---

[38] 9 U.N. GAOR, Gen. Comm. 8 (1954).
[39] 11 U.N. GAOR, 1st Comm. 221 (1956–7).
[40] Id. at 221.
[41] See 562 H.C. Deb. (5th ser.) 1267–79 (1956).

Turkish Cypriot population. Thus some 650 square miles would have become sovereign Turkish territory.

It seems most unlikely that the British seriously advanced the partition proposal as a sound solution. Cyprus is 'an ethnographical fruitcake in which the Greek and Turkish currants were mixed up in every town and village and often in every street'.[42] A massive population reallocation would have been required to separate Greek and Turkish Cypriots. The history of the Greek and Turkish transfers in the 1920s indicated that the human costs of such an effort would have been enormous. No one could have believed that such a solution would be favoured by Greek Cypriots. Rather, it seems most likely that the Solomon-like proposal to cut the island in two was a tactical step designed to neutralize the Greek appeal for self-determination. In simplest terms, the proposal seemed to offer something for both sides: Greek Cypriots should have the opportunity to determine their future; so should Turkish Cypriots. To make the point, the British did not have to extend the argument to the two per cent or three per cent of the Cypriot population that was neither Greek nor Turkish.

The Greek Government naturally objected to the suggestion of a bifurcated Cyprus. 'Cyprus as a whole was a living body. It could not be cut up without being killed.'[42] The scheme was 'an innovation which would be fraught with the most serious international implications and consequences'.[44] But Turkish representatives in the United Nations picked up the idea in 1957 and 1958 and made it their own. Cyprus was composed of two distinct peoples and if sovereignty were to be changed, the only issue was where to trace the boundary through the Island that would separate Greece and Turkey. '[I]n the case of Cyprus the use of the words "majority" and "minority" in a juridical or political context could not be justified under international law . . . those terms had been used to imply juridical consequences only in the case of constituted States or nations forming political entities.'[45] In fact, under Article 73 of the Charter, the United Kingdom was 'duty bound' to take into account the aspirations of the two communities.[46]

Greece presented an extensive series of legal arguments against

---

[42] Foley, *Legacy of Strife* 87 (1964).

[43] 11 U.N. GAOR, 1st Comm. 234 (1957).   [44] Ibid.

[45] 13 U.N. GAOR, 1st Comm. 256 (1958).   [46] Id. at 256.

partition, but each seemed only to weaken further its call for self-determination as the path to enosis. Once Turkey adopted the partition proposal, the British backed off somewhat. 'The United Kingdom was not in favour of partition, but the fact that partition was a solution advocated by some had to be taken into account.'[47] Law thus provided a tool for the British to manoeuvre themselves into precisely the public posture they presumably desired: a moderating influence between two opposing nations. At least in part, Britain appeared the honest broker trying to resolve conflict, not the source of conflict.

But these stratagems took a substantial toll on the credibility of the British position that its continued sovereignty was essential. At no time in the United Nation debates through 1958 did England's representatives declare a willingness to relinquish sovereignty at a date certain. But by 1957 they explicitly recognized that the time would come eventually. That year brought a new prime minister, Mr. Macmillan, into office, and he was anxious to resolve the matter as rapidly as possible. The only issue was when and under what circumstances.

As we have seen, Archbishop Makarios let it be known in 1958 that he was prepared to accept an independent Cyprus. No outsider can be sure why his position shifted so suddenly; independence had not been seriously discussed at length before in any public forum. But it seems likely that a major factor was the extent to which the legal basis for enosis was effectively blocked by the partition proposal. Reportedly, the Archbishop was seriously concerned that the British might actually go through with the scheme. When the British prime minister announced the so-called Macmillan Plan for the governance of Cyprus in June 1958,[48] British officials again suggested partition might be an ultimate solution; they were quite explicit that Turkey would

[47] Id. at 308.

[48] The Plan proposed that each community on the Island would govern its communal affairs through a separate House of Representatives. The Governor, representatives of Greece and Turkey, and Cypriots chosen by the two Houses would run the administration. Foreign affairs, defence matters, and internal security would be in the hands of the Governor, acting in consultation with Greek and Turkish representatives. An impartial tribunal would pass on any legislation alleged to be discriminatory by the Greek or Turkish Governments. Finally, a seven-year moratorium on consideration of the international status of Cyprus would be instituted to see how well the plan worked. See Cyprus: Statement of Policy, Cmnd. 455 (1958); Stephens, *Cyprus: A Place of Arms* 154–6 (1966).

have an absolute veto over any final arrangement. In all events, the international support necessary to pressure England into accepting enosis had been seriously undercut.

The Greek and Greek Cypriot arguments for self-determination were further weakened by the position India had maintained since the very outset of the United Nations debates:

The position of our Government is that we would support and we desire the establishment and independence according to the wishes of the people wherever possible. . . . If freedom and self-government were the issue, we would support the inscription of this item. . . . [T]here are three claimants. There is the United Kingdom, and Greece, and now Turkey. Very soon it may become a free-for-all! We therefore regard this island as the homeland of its peoples, entitled to nationhood and independence.[49]

India's voice was persuasive, because her size and population made her a leader of the developing countries, because India, too, was once a British colony, and because of her first-hand experience with the problems of partition. Many newly independent nations that might have otherwise supported the Greek view found the Indian position more compelling.

The arguments in the General Assembly for independence also must have had an impact on the British Government. After Makarios endorsed independence, Greece proposed that solution in the thirteenth Assembly, coupling it with proposed guarantees for the Turkish Cypriot minority. Although Turkish representatives objected, the only concern they expressed was that the Greek call for independence was a 'tactical rewording of its claim to *enosis*'.[50]

Most important, British officials said that their country had no objection to considering the eventual independence of Cyprus in tripartite negotiations with Greece and Turkey, though independence alone would not solve underlying problems. Having advanced, for some unspecified time in the future, an untenable plan of partition that would have transferred sovereignty, England would have been hardpressed to reject a much more reasonable arrangement that was in the British tradition of relinquishing sovereignty over other former colonies. Timing remained at issue, for Britain urged that a period of self-govern-

[49] 9 U.N. GAOR 59 (1954).
[50] 13 U.N. GAOR, 1st Comm. 254 (1958). For the Greek position see id. at 249.

ment should precede any decision on the future status of the
Island. Greece apparently did not object to this approach;
although the Greek proposal for Cypriot independence implied
an immediate British decision, it also included a period of self-
government before the actual transfer of sovereignty. When
Greek and Turkish representatives finally met in Zurich, however, they apparently saw no reason to wait.

(2) *The European Commission on Human Rights*. Alleged British
violations of human rights were a theme running through all the
Greek presentations to the United Nations on the Cyprus problem. The Governor of Cyprus and those under him were charged
in the General Assembly with torture, arbitrary arrests and detentions without trial, heavy collective fines on villages, whipping
children, and much more. The General Assembly offered a major
forum in which to make such allegations for the purpose of publicity. But the Assembly has no regular mechanism for investigating claims that human rights have been violated. It has occasionally established investigatory machinery, but only on an *ad hoc*
basis. Greece urged the Assembly to appoint a fact-finding committee of 'neutral and impartial' members to investigate British
atrocities,[51] but the proposal was never seriously considered.

In some situations the opportunity to make allegations without
the risk of investigation is precisely what a claimant wants. But
in this situation, Greece apparently believed that additional
pressures could be brought to bear on Britain by an international
agency with a fact-finding arm. The European Convention on
Human Rights provided that agency.

As we have seen, under the terms of the Convention, Greece
was required to prove only a prima facie violation. Since Britain
itself had notified the Secretary-General of the Council of
Europe that it was taking measures that derogated from its Convention obligations because of the state of emergency, Greece
probably had little difficulty in making the prima facie case. The
repressive measures formally adopted by British authorities in
Cyprus—exile of the Archbishop, capital punishment for possessing arms, curfews, and so forth—were a matter of public record.
Allegations of atrocities were easily available in newspaper
stories and the like. The Commission procedure had the practical
effect of making Britain prove that it had not violated the Convention. This was, for Greece, an ideal procedural posture.

[51] See 11 U.N. GAOR, 1st Comm. 234 (1956–7).

In June 1956, the Commission appointed an investigation sub-committee; over the next two years it visited the Island, investigated charges, and issued a confidential report. The Commission itself then filed majority and minority opinions with the Committee of Ministers of the Council of Europe. These opinions were also confidential. Greece submitted a second application in July 1957 alleging 49 cases of torture for which the United Kingdom Government was responsible. The Commission admitted 29 of these, excluding the others because local remedies had not been exhausted. Again, a subcommittee was formed to determine the facts. Before the Committee of Ministers reached a decision on either case, a settlement was concluded at the Zurich Conference. Greece and Britain then asked the Commission to close the cases. Although it was not bound to do so, the Commission agreed.

Presumably there was strong pressure within the Commission not to condemn a member-nation publicly. But the very existence of the charges for two and a half years must have influenced the British Government not only to rescind or relax measures complained of by Greece, but also to extricate itself from the Island altogether. At the very least, British efforts to deal with EOKA were complicated by the presence of an international body 'competent to decide whether [emergency] measures taken by a Party under Article 15 of the Convention had been taken to the extent strictly required by the exigencies of the situation'. Perhaps most significant, an adverse judgement by the Commission would have been a serious blow to England's public posture.

(3) *The North Atlantic Treaty Organization.* NATO was the third international organization that had a substantial impact on the British decision to renounce sovereignty over Cyprus. NATO's influence, however, was in mediation, not in the provision of a public forum to present a range of legal, political, and moral arguments—as in the General Assembly—or in the opportunity to press the international law counterpart of criminal charges before an investigating body—as in the European Commission on Human Rights.

Greece and Turkey were not original signatories of the NATO Treaty, but both became members in 1951.[52] The next year, the

[52] North Atlantic Treaty, T.I.A.S. No. 1964, 34 U.N.T.S. 243 (1949); Protocol to the North Atlantic Treaty on the Accession of Greece and Turkey, T.I.A.S. No. 2390, 126 U.N.T.S. 350 (1951). Article 5 of the Treaty provides

NATO South-East European command was established in Izmir, Turkey. From the outset of the Cyprus controversy in 1954, the United Kingdom argued that maintenance of full sovereignty was essential to fulfil its NATO obligations. Two major military bases were located on the Island. After the transfer of the British Middle Eastern Command to Cyprus in 1954, England claimed that 'Cyprus was an integral part of [the NATO] defence system and the United Kingdom had to have complete administrative authority there in order to ensure stability in the Middle East . . .'[53] Selwyn Lloyd stressed the range of United Kingdom treaty responsibilities, particularly to NATO, in declaring that 'Cyprus is vital to the discharge of those responsibilities . . . [T]here is no acceptable alternative in the circumstances to sovereignty. Full administrative control is necessary because leases expire, treaties have a habit of being whittled away and . . . Greek governments, like other governments, change.'[54] Britain's experience under the Anglo-Egyptian Treaty was obviously much in mind.

By 1957, however, British representatives were suggesting that there was room for compromise. England was 'under an obligation not to neglect the strategic responsibilities which it had assumed as a member of organizations of collective self-defence in accordance with Article 51 of the United Nations Charter'.[55] But these duties and interests left a margin of compromise. And, by 1958, the end was in sight. British strategic requirements in Cyprus did not constitute a serious obstacle to either an interim or a final solution. Not only were these requirements moderate and easily met, but they had been generally accepted by both Greece and Turkey as valuable and necessary to stability and security in the area. Throughout this period, pressures by and through NATO were an important element.

---

that 'an armed attack against one or more [of the Parties] . . . shall be considered an attack against them all . . . ' Article II of the Protocol expanded this provision to include an 'armed attack . . . on the forces, vessels or aircraft of any of the Parties, when in or over . . . the Mediterranean Sea . . .' For reasons that are not at all clear to the outside observer, however, an attack against Mediterranean islands under the jurisdiction of a Party is not covered under Article 5, unlike an attack against 'islands under the jurisdiction of any of the Parties in the North Atlantic area north of the Tropic of Cancer'.

[53] 9 U.N. GAOR, Gen. Comm. 9 (1954).

[54] 9 U.N. GAOR, 54 (1954).

[55] 12 U.N. GAOR, 1st Comm. 346 (1957).

In the initial stages of the controversy, these pressures were indirect, largely because Greece sought to exclude Cyprus as a matter for consideration within NATO. For several reasons, Greece viewed the United Nations as a preferable battleground. Most important, her obvious allies in calling for self-determination were the newly-independent developing nations. None of those countries was a member of NATO. Within that organization, only Iceland could be counted on for support. Further, military strategy received primary emphasis in NATO discussions. Viewed in strategic terms, the *status quo* was quite satisfactory, and substantially preferable to the uncertainties of self-determination and Greek–Turkish animosities. Finally, the public proceedings in the General Assembly offered a much better opportunity than the private NATO session to advertise the Greek Cypriot position to the world.

NATO in fact had no formal conciliation procedure for handling disputes among member-states until 1956. This made it initially difficult for England to press an argument in favour of resolving the matter within that organization. After 1956, Greece effectively claimed that the United Nations was seized of the matter and that the NATO discussions could not oust it from its primary jurisdiction.

Although Greece did not choose to resolve the Cyprus problem within NATO, the Greek Government did take several steps to encourage NATO members, particularly the United States, to bring pressure on Britain. In September 1955, Greece refused to participate in NATO manoeuvres, and when Archbishop Makarios was deported six months later, Greek air and naval bases were closed to British and Turkish forces. Greek troops were also withdrawn from the NATO base at Izmir, Turkey. And domestic discontent in Greece as a result of the Cyprus problem was a principal reason for the Greek Government's refusal to allow NATO nuclear bases on Greek territory. Greece did not resume full co-operation with other NATO forces in the Eastern Mediterranean until the Archbishop was released in 1957.[56]

Turkey also withdrew its troops from their NATO commitments on several occasions during this period in response to—perhaps in retaliation against—Greek actions. Further, the strained relations between Greece and Turkey were a primary

[56] Royal Institute of International Affairs, *Cyprus: the Dispute and Settlement* 35 (1959).

cause of the collapse of the Balkan Pact, the principal link between NATO and Yugoslavia.[57] All these pressures took a serious
toll on the unity of NATO. A breach in the organization's
southern flank was rapidly expanding. The United States was
particularly concerned, and exerted substantial pressures on the
United Kingdom—as well as Greece and Turkey—to resolve the
controversy. The strategic rationale for maintaining sovereignty
over Cyprus was undercut to the extent that British forces on the
Island were occupied with internal rebellion and the rift in the
alliance weakened the common front against the Soviet Union.
All this was apparently part of the Greek design to use NATO
to pressurize the United Kingdom and Turkey to accept enosis.
Although the scheme did not ultimately succeed, it must have
weakened British resolve to remain on the Island, particularly in
the initial period of the controversy from 1954 to 1956.

At the same time, the controversy was one of the stimuli that
led to the creation of a Committee of Three in May 1956. The
Committee was 'to advise the Council on ways and means to
improve and extend NATO co-operation in non-military fields
and to develop greater unity within the Atlantic Community'.[58]
Six months later the Committee proposed a new set of arrangements to deal with intra-organization political disputes.[59] First,
all such controversies not resolved by direct negotiations should
be submitted to NATO procedures before resort to other international organizations. Second, every member and the Secretary-
General should have the right and obligation to bring any disputes that threatened the 'solidarity or effectiveness' of NATO
directly to the NATO Council. Finally, the Secretary-General
should offer his good offices to disputing parties and, if they
agreed, should 'initiate or facilitate procedures of inquiry,
mediation, conciliation, or arbitration'. A ministerial meeting of
the Council subsequently adopted these proposals.

As a result of the new arrangements, NATO was in a position
to try to resolve the Cyprus dispute. The United Kingdom representatives said it would accept NATO mediation if Greece withdrew its appeal to the United Nations. Greece, however, had
accepted the new procedures with the reservation that they

[57] See Ball, *NATO and the European Union Movement* 142 (1959).

[58] Baumann, *Political Cooperation in NATO* 20 (1960).

[59] Non-military Cooperation in NATO: Text of Report of the Committee
of Three (Dec. 1956), 5 NATO Letter, Special supplement to No. 1, 1 Jan. 1957.

would not apply to matters already before another international body. Greece had the Cyprus dispute very much in mind in stipulating the reservation, and maintained its position. Nonetheless, the NATO Secretary-General offered his good offices for conciliation in early 1957. As might have been expected, the United Kingdom and Turkey accepted the offer, but Greece rejected it. Greek representatives were reportedly increasingly concerned that NATO mediation would lead to partition—a solution that seemed to offer something for all sides. They claimed, therefore, that they could not consider the problem outside the United Nations since that body was seized of the matter, and that England was obliged to negotiate directly with the Cypriots under the 1956 General Assembly resolution.

In 1957, as terrorist activities within the Island increased and the rift between Greece and Turkey deepened, the new NATO Secretary-General, Paul Henri Spaak, again tried to bring the parties together.[60] His proposed settlement, as ultimately worked out, was essentially a modification of the plan put forth by Mr. Macmillan. For a brief period, Greece expressed a willingness to accept the proposal as a basis for negotiations, apparently in an effort to stave off implementation of the Macmillan Plan. But British officials made it clear that their own scheme would be put into effect, and Greece returned again to the United Nations.

Each of these efforts within NATO must have made it more evident to the United Kingdom that its NATO allies were becoming increasingly restive at the festering sore affecting the organization's defensive strength. At the same time, the failure of both Mr. Spaak's proposals and the Macmillan Plan also made it clear that 'limited self-government' with continued British rule did not provide a basis for a settlement. Some new solution was essential. An independent Cyprus provided that solution.

[60] Discussion on Cyprus in the North Atlantic Treaty Organization, Sept.–Oct. 1958, Cmnd. 566 (1958).

III

THE CYPRIOT GOVERNMENT'S DECISION IN 1963 TO PROPOSE REVISIONS OF THE ZURICH–LONDON SETTLEMENT

THE negotiating efforts of the Greek and Turkish Governments, that began with a meeting of their United Nations representatives in late 1958, culminated in a Zurich conference of the two prime ministers, Karamanlis and Menderes, during February 1959. That meeting was followed by another in London, where Greek and Turkish officials were joined by representatives of the United Kingdom and the two communities on the Island. These two conferences worked out arrangements for Cypriot independence, subject to the terms of a series of interrelated agreements known as the Zurich–London Accords. In November 1963, the President of the Cypriot Republic, Archbishop Makarios, proposed a series of revisions in one of those Accords, the Constitution of the Republic.[1] This section considers the ways in which the

---

[1] Makarios, 'Proposals To Amend the Cyprus Constitution', International Relations (Athens), Apr. 1964, pp. 8–25. The proposed revisions were as follows:

'1. The right of veto of the President and the Vice-President of the Republic should be abandoned.

'2. The Vice-President of the Republic should deputise for the President of the Republic in case of his temporary absence or incapacity to perform his duties.

'3. The Greek President of the House of Representatives and the Turkish Vice-President should be elected by the House as a whole and not as at present the President by the Greek Members of the House and the Vice-President by the Turkish Members of the House.

'4. The Vice-President of the House of Representatives should deputise for the President of the House in case of his temporary absence or incapacity to perform his duties.

'5. The constitutional provisions regarding separate majorities for enactment of certain laws by the House of Representatives should be abolished.

'6. Unified Municipalities should be established.

'7. The administration of Justice should be unified.

malfunctioning of the Island's internal legal system led to the
decision and the role of law in the external pressures that apparently precluded alternative decisions.

The Cypriot Constitution is the linchpin of the 1960 settlement.[2] By its terms, the President must be a Greek Cypriot, and
the Vice-President a Turkish Cypriot, each elected by his own
community. Their executive powers are essentially co-terminous.
Each can block important actions of the other. The Attorney-
General and his deputy and the two chief administrators in
other major executive offices must also be chosen from different
communities. A ten-man Council of Ministers holds all residual
executive power. The President designates seven members; the
Vice-President three. Legislative authority is vested in a House of
Representatives. Its members are elected seventy per cent from
the Greek Cypriot community and thirty per cent from the
Turkish Cypriot community. The civil service must also maintain its membership in that same proportion, the army in a 60–40
ratio. Institutional protection of Turkish Cypriot interests is
built into the Constitution through required representation at
every level of the Government and Turkish veto power over
critical decisions in most areas. They key or 'basic' constitutional
provisions 'cannot, in any way, be amended, whether by way of
variation, addition or repeal'. Other provisions can be revised
only with the approval of two-thirds of the Representatives from
each community. Almost every one of the 199 Articles in the
Constitution was drafted with a view to maintaining a delicate
but immutable equilibrium between the interests of the Greek

'8. The division of the Security Forces into Police and Gendarmerie should
be abolished.

'9. The numerical strength of the Security Forces and of the Defence Forces
should be determined by a Law.

'10. The proportion of the participation of Greek and Turkish Cypriots in
the composition of the Public Service and the Forces of the Republic should
be modified in proportion to the ratio of the population of Greek and Turkish
Cypriots.

'11. The number of the Members of the Public Service Commission should
be reduced from ten to five.

'12. All decisions of the Public Service Commission should be taken by simple
majority.

'13. The Greek Communal Chamber should be abolished.'

[2] The terms of the Constitution and the other 1960 Accords are analysed in
some detail in Kyriakides, *Cyprus: Constitutionalism and Crisis Government* 53–71
(1968).

majority and the Turkish minority. Communal distrust permeates the entire document.

But the 1960 settlement did not depend on the Constitution alone. If the constitutional guarantees in favour of the Turkish Cypriots were violated, international guarantees were to become operative. By the Treaty of Guarantee, Cyprus, Greece, Turkey, and the United Kingdom undertake to prohibit all activity tending to promote 'directly or indirectly either union [with Greece] . . . or partition of the Island'. Cyprus also promises to ensure 'respect for its Constitution', and Greece, Turkey, and the United Kingdom recognize and guarantee not only the 'independence, territorial integrity and security of the Republic of Cyprus', but also 'the state of affairs established by the Basic [unamendable] Articles of the Constitution'. In the event of a breach of the treaty, the Guarantor Powers are to consult together, but 'in so far as common or concerted action may prove impossible', each reserves 'the right to take action with the sole aim of re-establishing the state of affairs established by the present Treaty'. A second agreement, the Treaty of Alliance, calls for co-operative measures by the Cypriot, Greek, and Turkish Governments to protect the Island, including a permanent tripartite military headquarters with 950 Greek and 650 Turkish troops. A third Accord, the Treaty of Establishment, declares that England retains sovereignty over two military-base areas totalling 99 square miles.

It is tempting to say that the scheme never had any chance of lasting success—that a constitution requiring the ethnic origin of the coroner in a coroner's inquest to be that of the deceased could only fail. The documents of the 1960 settlement are incredibly detailed, often repetitious, and occasionally ambiguous. Despite substantial weaknesses, the settlement did represent an imaginative resolution of many difficult problems. Given patience and a spirit of compromise on each side, it might have worked. It is not a model of draftsmanship; but, viewing the circumstances, no more could have been expected. There was general agreement, however, that substantial goodwill would be needed on the part of both communities to make the arrangements work. As we shall see, what goodwill remained in 1960 among Greek and Turkish Cypriots was dissipated by the fall of 1963. Substantial cracks appeared in the unity between the two communities. As a result, key governmental operations came to

a virtual halt. On vital issues of taxation, the army, the civil service, and municipal responsibilities, Greek and Turkish Cypriots
were at an impasse.

In the eyes of Archbishop Makarios and most Greek Cypriots,
the problems facing the Island in the fall of 1963 were inherent
in the 1960 Accords and in the strictures they imposed on the
majority's freedom to govern. Those strictures will become more
evident in the discussion of the Accords in operation. At this
point, it is enough to characterize the problem as the Archbishop
saw it, and to suggest the range of alternatives open to him.

The evident desire of the Archbishop by 1963, and no doubt
even before, was to terminate the entire 1960 settlement and to
devise a new arrangement that would eliminate both some
Turkish Cypriot power and all authority of the Guarantor
Powers over the Island's destiny. Unilateral abrogation of all the
Accords was at one end of the spectrum of possible decisions open
to the Archbishop in response to the crisis. At the other end was
a decision to do nothing except renew efforts to work wholly
within the framework of the Accords. Somewhere in the middle
were a range of possible revisions of some or all of the Accords.
Such revisions could have been proposed in various ways and in
various forums.

The issue was resolved in November 1963 when the Archbishop
sent a memorandum to Vice-President Kutchuk proposing
thirteen revisions of the Constitution. 'Information' copies of the
memorandum were sent to the British, Greek, and Turkish
Governments. A few of the changes, such as authorizing the
Vice-President to act for the President in the event of the latter's
temporary absence or incapacity, would actually have provided
the Turkish Cypriots with more protection than before. But seven
revisions would have amended 'unamendable' (basic) articles for
which the Turks had fought hard at Zurich and London, including the Vice-President's power to veto, the requirement of
separate majorities in the House for passage of important legisla-
lation, separate municipalities, a limited security force, and
assurance of thirty per cent representation in the public service
and forty per cent in the army.

In analysing the role of law in framing the issue for decision
and in resolving it, this section follows the pattern established in
examining the British 1958 decision. Several critical differences
in the two situations, however, need emphasis. First, in so far as

an outside observer can determine, Archbishop Makarios was *the* decision-maker in a sense that was not true of any other leader discussed in this essay. Obviously, the Archbishop had advisers, and Macmillan did not delegate authority to decide the Cyprus issue in 1958. But a combination of circumstances makes it appropriate to characterize the Archbishop as the Cypriot Government on this issue in a way that no British prime minister can claim to have represented the British Government on any issue since World War II. First, the charismatic character of the Archbishop's leadership makes collective decision-making within the Cypriot Government unlikely. He has often been accused of being his own Rasputin but never of having another. Second, the issue in 1963 polarized the Island's two communities, and this process further focused key decisions in the hands of the Archbishop. Finally, this decision, in particular, went to the heart of the Cypriot Government's future; Cyprus in 1958 was important to the British, but hardly critical.

Another difference between decisions of the British Government in 1958 and the Cypriot Government in 1963 was the nature of the pressures by foreign governments and international arrangements. In the 1950s, the pressures on England built up over time, and were both explicit and public. Britain was on the defensive and was reacting to those pressures. There were, of course, numerous confidential sessions between British representatives and officials from other governments. The details of some of these negotiations remain hidden from public view. But the main lines of the approaches by Greece, Turkey, and the two Cypriot communities are evident. These approaches were publicly made over a substantial period of time before the decision.

In deciding the 1963 issue, Archbishop Makarios consulted Greek Government officials, and probably British representatives as well. He also obviously discussed the matter with Vice-President Kutchuk. But he was taking the initiative. The primary external pressures probably emerged more from expectations concerning how foreign governments would react to alternative decisions rather than from their fully articulated arguments on how the issue should be resolved. The difference is one of degree, not of kind, but it has significant consequences for the analysis here. The Turkish, British, and Greek Governments, and the various international arrangements potentially involved, were important to the Archbishop's decision primarily because of their probable reactions. No one could have been certain what those reactions would be, and the Archbishop never made public his own predictions. In large measure, therefore, analysis of the role of law in shaping the Archbishop's decision through pressures by foreign governments and international institutions is speculation about the Archbishop's speculations. To the extent that the analysis has value, it is to indicate the *kinds* of ways in which law *could have* been significant in the decision-making process.

There are other differences inherent in the situations in 1963 and 1958. As head of a sovereign state in 1963, for example, the Archbishop had ready and direct access to the United Nations; lack of such access was a major problem in the 1950s. Further, the Turkish Cypriot community and its leader, Dr. Kutchuk, were no longer juridically equal in international eyes to the Greek Cypriot community and its leader. These and other differences have a direct bearing on any effort to judge the comparative impact of law on the two decisions.

Much of the following analysis concerns the provisions of the 1960 settlement and implementation of the Accords through 1963. In part, the Archbishop's decision was triggered by the breakdown of the legal structure established at Zurich and London. Examination of that structure and its disintegration is, therefore, critical to understanding the impact of law in the decision-making process. The analysis then turns to the external pressures that were brought to bear on the process through foreign governments and international arrangements.

THE 1960 ACCORDS IN OPERATION: 1960–3

For about two and a half years, the 1960 settlement worked reasonably well. The constitutional machinery for keeping the peace between Greek and Turkish Cypriots did just that. The operation of the Supreme Constitutional Court is a good example and also offers an interesting illustration of some of the difficulties faced on the Island after more than seventy years of British rule. The Constitution calls for three judges on the Court—one Greek Cypriot, one Turkish Cypriot, and a neutral President. The neutral judge must be chosen jointly by the Republic's President and Vice-President. Archbishop Makarios and Dr. Kutchuk agreed on Professor Ernest Forsthoff, a leading German scholar in constitutional and administrative law from the University of Heidelberg. Professor Forsthoff faced a series of difficult problems when he arrived in Cyprus in September 1960. He was trained in the civil law, and some of the concepts in the Constitution are more akin to civil-law traditions than those of common law. But most of the lawyers on the Island had practised solely in the English courts of colonial Cyprus and were used to common-law traditions and methods. Furthermore, substantial bodies of law had developed in each of the communities that were quite different both from each other and, in many respects, from either the common or the civil law.[3]

Among the first issues the Court had to face was whether to adopt the common-law tradition of dissenting opinions or to follow the civil-law practice of issuing a single opinion of the Court. Professor Forsthoff urged the Greek and Turkish judges to follow the civil-law custom on the theory that, entirely apart from the merits of the issue as an abstract matter, dissenting opinions would weaken the Court's ability to lessen friction between the two communities. In disputes involving both Turkish and Greek parties, the community whose party lost would inevitably expect an impassioned dissent by the judge from that community, and this could only make the Court's job more difficult. This reasoning prevailed, and in over one hundred cases the Court filed unanimous opinions. Many of those suits involved significant issues between Greeks and Turks, and for a time the Court acted as an important moderating influence.[4]

[3] The history in this and the following paragraph was recounted to me by Dr. Edgar Kull of the University of Heidelberg, who was a legal assistant to Professor Forsthoff during a portion of his term as President of the Supreme Constitutional Court.

[4] The Court's independence during this period is illustrated by its decision concerning a supplementary appropriations statute to provide funds for the two Communal Chambers. See Vice-President of the Republic, and the House of Representatives, Supreme Constitutional Court, 14 Dec 1961, 2 Reports of the Supreme Constitutional Court of Cyprus 144 [hereinafter cited as R.S.C.C.]. Article 88 of the Constitution requires a minimum allocation to the Chambers of £2 million, in a ratio of 4–1, but authorizes increases above that amount, allocated 'in such manner as the House of Representatives may decide'. The Vice-President referred the statute to the Court under Article 138, charging that it unconstitutionally discriminated against the Turkish Cypriot community. The House denied the allegation of unconstitutional discrimination, presumably on the basis that Article 88 grants to the House exclusive jurisdiction over the matter. Furthermore, the House claimed that the issue was improperly before the Court since Article 138 concerns the budget only, and the statute was not part of the budget. (The Vice-President could have avoided

The first overt sign that all was not in perfect harmony on the Island occurred in the spring of 1961, when the Turkish Cypriots expressed increasing concern that the public service was not being filled in a 70–30 ratio as required by the Constitution. In retaliation, the Turkish members of the House of Representatives refused to support an extension of the Island's tax laws. The President, however, ordered taxes to be collected under the pre-1960 income-tax law, on the ground that the right to a separate vote on tax matters did not include 'the right to use this privilege over other unconnected demands'.[5] In February 1963, the Supreme Constitutional Court ruled that the pre-1960 law was no longer in force and that there was, therefore, no machinery for the assessment or collection of taxes.[6]

Later that same year the Council of Ministers voted to establish an army in which soldiers from the two communities would be integrated. But Dr. Kutchuk vetoed this decision, as was his right under the Constitution, on the ground that an integrated army would be unable to function. As a result Archbishop Makarios announced that he would not establish an army at all.[7]

In the wake of these controversies the Archbishop gave the first indication that he would not acquiesce in Turkish Cypriot vetoes

---

this problem by bringing his action under Article 137, which applies to any law or decision of the House that is allegedly discriminatory.) The Court agreed that the statute was not part of the budget, but none the less went on to hold the statute unconstitutional on the ground not of discrimination but of invalid procedure in adoption. In introducing the legislation to the House, the Council of Ministers had included an allocation provision, and the Court held that this violated the implied requirement in Article 88(2) that the House consider the issue of allocation as an independent body.

There is little to be said in favour of such a strict interpretation of the Constitution's separation of powers. The Court itself stated that although the Council could not incorporate an allocation in the bill it introduced in the House, it could recommend an allocation 'in appropriate terms'. Id. at 148. Such a distinction seems wholly unnecessary in terms of the practical operations of government. But the decision is a perfect example of the way the Court sought, as a completely independent body, to resolve intercommunal problems.

[5] *Observer* (London), 2 Apr. 1961, p. 4, col. 1.

[6] Vasos Constantinou Kyriakides, and the Republic of Cyprus, Supreme Constitutional Court, 8 Feb 1963, 4 R.S.C.C. 109.

[7] See *The Times* (London), 23 Oct. 1961, p. 9, col. 5. The Constitution provides that the 2,000-man army shall be made up of 60 per cent of Greek Cypriots and 40 per cent of Turkish Cypriots, but it does not specify whether the communal contingents are to be integrated.

over the decisions of the majority, even though they were in
accordance with the provisions of the Constitution. In January
1962 he charged that the Zurich–London Agreements conferred
rights on the Turkish Cypriots 'beyond what is just' to protect
them, and 'since the Turkish minority abuses these constitutional
rights and creates obstacles to the smooth functioning of the state,
I am obliged to disregard, or seek revision of, those provisions
which obstruct the state machinery and which, if abused, endanger the very existence of the state'.[8]

Three key requirements were at issue: the 70–30 ratio in the
public service, separate majorities in the House of Representatives for all tax bills, and separate Turkish municipalities in the
five largest towns. It was the third issue, more than any other,
that proved the major problem.

The Archbishop and the Greek Cypriot majority in the House
refused from the outset to establish separate Turkish Cypriot
municipalities in these towns, presumably on the ground that
this would give the Turkish Cypriots too much authority on the
local level. The issue came to a head at the beginning of 1963
when the Council of Ministers invoked a pre-independence
statute and declared that the five towns were 'improvement
areas' to be governed by special boards established by the Council.[9] Under this arrangement Turkish Cypriots would have had
no control over the administration of their own sectors of the
towns.

In response, the Turkish Communal Chamber both adopted
its own 'Turkish Municipal Law' and applied to the Supreme
Constitutional Court for a ruling that the Council's order was
void. On 25 April 1963, the Court upheld the Chamber's application on the ground, among others, that the Council's order
violated the constitutional requirement that separate municipalities be established in the five towns.[10]

For the first time, the Greek Cypriot judge dissented. The contention that one of the Constitution's basic articles could be cir-
cumvented by the simple device of failing to establish municipali-

[8] Id., 5 Jan. 1962, p. 10, col. 5.

[9] See id., 3 Jan. 1963, p. 7, col. 3, id., 1 Jan. 1963, p. 9, col. 5. The statute
invoked was the Villager (Administration and Improvement) Law, *The Statute
Laws of Cyprus*, c. 243, §4 (1959).

[10] The Turkish Communal Chamber and the Council of Ministers, Supreme
Constitutional Court, 25 Apr. 1963, 5 R.S.C.C. 59, 74–7.

ties seems absurd in view of the significance the Turkish Cypriots attached to the provision. Nevertheless the dissent, after more than two years of unanimity, was obvious evidence of increasing differences between the two communities.

On the same day, the Court ruled that the Turkish Communal Chamber's 'Turkish Municipal Law' was also unconstitutional because the Chamber could act concerning municipalities only 'after general legislation of the House of Representatives concerning the municipalities . . . has been made'.[11] The Turkish judge dissented in this case. He had become, like his Greek Cypriot counterpart, a public advocate for his community's position.

Tensions rapidly built up through the summer and autumn of 1963. On 3 December the Archbishop publicly announced his thirteen proposed revisions of the Constitution. Dr. Kutchuk apparently had agreed to consider them. But before he commented on the substance, the Turkish Government rejected them outright. The Archbishop refused the rejection. Within days, the fighting began.[12]

As one commentator wrote, 'A trivial incident sparked the outbreak, but the tinder was dry and plenty of fuel lay to hand.' Two Greek Cypriot policemen, according to his report, 'asked some Turkish Cypriots to produce their identity cards. The Turks refused; an argument followed, and a crowd began to gather. The policemen, finding themselves surrounded, drew their guns. Shots were fired, it seems, by both sides. Two Turks were killed and a policeman seriously injured.'[13] The next day fighting broke out all over Nicosia and quickly spread to other parts of the Island.

A Christmas Eve peace call by both Archbishop Makarios and Dr. Kutchuk failed to stop the bloodshed. A similar call by the British, Greek, and Turkish Governments was also unsuccessful. Turkish jet-fighters flew low over Nicosia, and rumours of an imminent Turkish invasion spread throughout the Island. Cyprus had, within a matter of days, become the focus of an international crisis.

The malfunctioning of the Island's internal legal system was

[11] The House of Representatives, and the Turkish Communal Chamber, Supreme Constitutional Court, 25 Apr. 1963, 5 R.S.C.C. 123, 128.

[12] See *The Times* (London), 7 Dec. 1963, p. 7, col. 3; id., 24 Dec. 1963, p. 6, col. 6. See also 18 U.N. SCOR, 1085th meeting 8–9 (1963).

[13] Foley, *Legacy of Strife: Cyprus From Rebellion to Civil War* 166–168 (1964).

obviously a major pressure on the Archbishop to alter the arrangements concluded in 1960. But there were considerable countervailing forces of law. Unlike the British decision described in Chapter II, those forces primarily came from outside the Island, particularly from Turkey. At the least, they influenced the Archbishop's judgements not simply to abrogate the 1960 settlement or even to call for revision of all the Accords. Instead, he proposed only modifications of the one document most closely concerned with the Island's internal affairs.[14] Those modifications would deal with the most immediate concerns of governmental stalemate. They would also minimize the risks of adverse international reactions that could undermine the long-run success of any effort to change the *status quo*.

The legal position of the Cypriot Government, as later articulated in the United Nations, was that the 'Constitution was foisted on Cyprus . . . The combined effect of the Constitution and the Treaty of Guarantee is that a situation has been created whereby the constitutional and political development of the Republic has been arrested in its infancy and the Republic as a sovereign State has been placed in a strait jacket.'[15] The resulting legal conclusion was that to the extent the 1960 Accords precluded amendment of the Constitution, they were 'unequal and inequitable treaties, as a result of which they cannot be regarded as anything but null and void'.[16]

In support of the Cypriot position, some nations have contended that 'unequal' treaties—agreements imposing burdens on states in substantially unequal bargaining positions—are

[14] As discussed in Chapter IV, Turkey subsequently threatened military intervention under the treaty to enforce the terms of the 1960 settlement. In response, Cypriot representatives claimed that the Treaty of Guarantee was invalid. Later, they also maintained that the Cypriot Government had terminated the Treaty of Alliance because of an alleged breach by Turkey, as discussed in Chapter V. But at the outset, Cypriot claims were limited to the Constitution and the need for its revision.

According to Stephens, *Cyprus, A Place of Arms* 185–6 (1966), the Cypriot Government did announce on 1 Jan. 1964, that it had abrogated the Treaties of Alliance and Guarantee. Mr. Stephens reports that immediately after the announcement, British representatives convinced Archbishop Makarios that the move was a mistake, and a new statement was issued declaring that the Cypriot Government sought no more than 'to secure the termination of these treaties by appropriate means'.

[15] 19 U.N. SCOR, 1098th meeting 20 (1964).

[16] 20 U.N. SCOR, 1235th meeting 25 (1964).

per se void.[17] According to this argument, coercion is a ground for invalidating treaties, and states are 'coerced' when they conclude agreements from substantially unequal bargaining positions.

If such a qualification on *pacta sunt servanda* is accepted, it follows—at least arguably—that the 1960 Accords were 'unequal' since Cyprus was not an independent nation when the Agreements were negotiated, and a settlement acceptable to the British was a condition of independence. Furthermore, Greek Cypriot and Turkish Cypriot representatives had no negotiating role in the Zurich Conference, where the basic structure of the Accords was established. Although they were present at the London Conference where the details of the settlement were worked out, they had not been elected as representatives by the Cypriot people.[18] More important, the choice offered Archbishop Makarios and Dr. Kutchuk was essentially to take the settlement or to refuse it. At the conclusion of the Conference, the agreement was sealed by a memorandum signed on behalf of the three Governments. The memorandum took 'note' of declarations by Archbishop Makarios and Dr. Kutchuk that they 'accept the documents [signed at the Conference] . . . as the agreed founda-

[17] This is the view of a number of Soviet writers. See *International Law, A Textbook for Use in Law Schools* 248 (Academy of Sciences of the U.S.S.R., Institute of State and Law, Kozhevnikov (ed.), Ogden (trans.), no date); Talalayev and Boyarshinov, 'Unequal Treaties as a Mode of Prolonging the Colonial Dependence of the New States of Asia and Africa', [1961] Soviet Yearbook of International L. 169. See generally McWhinney, '"Peaceful Coexistence" and Soviet-Western International Law', 56 Am. J. Int'l L. 951, 957 (1962). The United Nations debate concerning the French occupation of a military base at Bizerta includes a number of statements by other nations in support of this position. See, e.g., U.N. GAOR, 3d Spec. Sess., Plenary 63–4 (A/PV. 1002) (1961) (statement by the representative of Guinea). See generally Lester, 'Bizerta and the Unequal Treaty Theory', 11 Int'l & Comp. L.Q. 847 (1962).

[18] The subsequent elections in Dec. 1959 indicate, however, that Archbishop Makarios and Dr. Kutchuk would have been selected if the Cypriot people had been able to make a choice.

Furthermore, the Greek and Turkish Governments probably believed that they adequately represented the Island's two communities, a view that was apparently shared by most Turkish Cypriot as well as by the British. And, as we have seen, there is much in history to support this judgement. But should such representation be considered as meeting the minimum standards of self-determination? The question is troublesome, for there is as little accord on the content of those standards as on the appropriate occasions for the exercise of the Charter right of self-determination.

tion for the final settlement of the problem of Cyprus'.[19] But their only available alternative was rejection; they could not bargain over the settlement's content. On these grounds, the Cypriot Government could charge that '[t]hese treaties which contained onerous provisions were thus imposed on the majority of the people of Cyprus making the doctrine of unequal, inequitable and unjust treaties relevant.'[20]

Cypriot representatives never pressed this position, however, to its logical conclusion: that the entire 1960 settlement was void. In part, the reason may have been concern that Turkey and the United Kingdom would respond that if the settlement was invalid then Cyprus was still a British colony. But no one seriously urged that position; the Republic of Cyprus had been a member of the United Nations for over three years and its 'sovereign equality' was recognized by the Charter. Much more important, there were strong pressures from at least Turkey and England, and probably Greece as well, against abrogation of all the Accords. In large part, those pressures were framed in legal terms.

A. PRESSURES FROM TURKEY AND THE TURKISH CYPRIOTS

Protection of rights won under the Zurich–London settlement was the principal concern of Turkish Cypriots and, therefore, of Turkey. As in 1957, there were substantial domestic pressures within Turkey to support and protect Turkish Cypriots. In May 1960 a small group of young army officers had led a bloodless coup that overthrew the government of the prime minister, Menderes, and his Democratic Party. Some reports have suggested that dissatisfaction with the Zurich–London settlement was one of the factors that triggered the coup, though domestic issues were more important. A new constitution was adopted in 1961, and elections were held in the fall of that year. The Democratic Party was dissolved, three of its key leaders including Mr. Menderes were hanged, and others imprisoned. In the elections, the People's Party won a plurality, but the new Justice Party—which included many former Democrats—was a close second. During the next three years, the threat of intervention by the armed forces was always a possibility, although the People's Party had the tacit backing of the military. Unsuccessful take-

[19] Conference of Cyprus, Documents Signed and Initialled at Lancaster House, Cmd. 679, at 4 (1959).
[20] 19 U.N. SCOR, 1098th meeting 20 (1965).

over attempts by young army officers in both 1962 and 1963 underscored the point. The political situation was made more difficult because the government under Mr. Inonu was formed by a series of coalitions. The People's Party always dominated, but it never had a majority in the legislature.

The case in support of the validity of the 1960 Accords was a substantial one, though by no means unclouded. The traditional view of international legal theorists is that 'a treaty is not rendered *ipso facto* void, or voidable by one of the parties, by reason of the fact that such party was coerced by the other party into concluding it, whether that coercion is applied at the time of signature or of ratification or at both times.'[21] The International Law Commission's draft Convention on the Law of Treaties, as published in 1963, went several steps further: 'Any treaty the conclusion of which was procured by the threat or use of force in violation of the principle of the Charter of the United Nations shall be void.'[22] This formulation tries to strike a balance between the importance of maintaining treaty obligations on the one hand and the obvious requirement that international agreements be concluded in a manner consistent with the Charter on the other. But even on the basis of the Commission's prescript, Turkey could properly conclude that the Cypriot contention could not be sustained. Although violence was part of the Island's daily diet for decades before the 1960 settlement was concluded, the settlement was not procured by force.

[21] McNair, *The Law of Treaties* 208 (1965). Lord McNair was referring to 'coercion applied to the State itself, not . . . personal intimidation applied to its representative'. Id. at 208–9. See also Harvard Research in International Law, 'Law of Treaties', Part III, 29 Am. J. Int'l L. Spec. Supp. 653, 657 (1935).

[22] International Law Commission, Draft Law of Treaties, Art. 36, U.N. Doc. No. A/5509, at 10 (1963). The draft was adopted with some minor modifications and renumbering of articles at a 1969 conference in Vienna. For the final text, see U.N. Doc. A/Conf. 39/27 (1969); 63 Am. J. Int'l L. 875 (1969).

The General Assembly adopted a 'Declaration of the Prohibition of Military, Political or Economic coercion in the Conclusion of Treaties' at the same time it adopted the Convention on the Law of Treaties. See U.N. Doc. No. A/7697, Annex at 1 (1969). The Declaration 'solemnly condemns the threat or use of pressure in any form, whether military, political, or economic, by any State in order to coerce another State to perform any act relating to the conclusion of a treaty in violation of the principles of the sovereign equality of States and freedom of consent'. Article 36 of the Commission's 1963 draft became Article 52 in the Convention as adopted by the General Assembly. See U.N. Doc. A/Conf. 39/27 (1969).

Moreover, there has been substantial controversy concerning the willingness with which Archbishop Makarios, leader of the Greek Cypriot delegation at the 1959 London Conference, signed the Agreements. At the closing ceremonies he stated: 'Yesterday I had certain reservations. In overcoming them I have done so in a spirit of trust and good-hearted good will towards the Turkish community and its leaders. It is my firm belief that with sincere understanding and mutual confidence we can work together in a way that will leave no room for dissension about any written provisions and guarantees. It is the spirit in the hearts of men that counts most. I am sure that all past differences will be completely forgotten.'[23] Writing four years later, however, he stated:

At the Conference at Lancaster House in February, 1959, which I was invited to attend as leader of the Greek Cypriots, I raised a number of objections and expressed strong misgivings regarding certain provisions of the Agreement arrived at in Zurich between the Greek and the Turkish Governments and adopted by the British Government. I tried very hard to bring about the change of at least some provisions of that Agreement. I failed, however, in that effort and I was faced with the dilemma either of signing the Agreement as it stood or of rejecting it with all the grave consequences which would have ensued. In the circumstances I had no alternative but to sign the Agreement. This was the course dictated to me by necessity.[24]

It may be that the Archbishop's former statement minimized his 'reservations' out of respect for his co-signatories; but it seems equally plausible that his latter statement overemphasized his 'misgivings' in an effort to justify his current views concerning the 1960 Accords.

In all events, Turkey could properly claim that a requirement of absolute equality in bargaining power would mean that almost every treaty between developed and developing nations would be void. Such a qualification on the principle that international agreements must be observed would make the principle virtually meaningless. It is impossible to do more than speculate on the impact that weaknesses in the 'inequality' case had on Greek Cypriot officials. But those weaknesses, and the potential inter-

[23] Conference on Cyprus, Final Statements at Closing Plenary Session at Lancaster House, Cmnd. 680, at 6 (Document XXX) (1959).
[24] Makarios, 'Proposals to Amend the Cyprus Constitution', International Relations (Athens), Apr. 1964, p. 8.

national support for the Turkish position on the matter, was presumably one reason why the Archbishop did not carry through a complete renunciation of the 1960 Accords.[25]

Looming over other potential Turkish reactions to a decision by the Archbishop was the possibility of Turkish military intervention under Article IV of the Treaty of Guarantee. That provision authorized each Guarantor Power, after consultation with the others, 'to take action with the sole aim of re-establishing the state of affairs created by the present Treaty'. Article IV is analysed in some detail in the next chapter. That analysis supports the view that 'action' under Article IV may, in some circumstances, properly include the use of force. The issue here is not whether those circumstances were actually present in the fall of 1963, but rather Archbishop Makarios's view of the risk of Turkish armed intervention. That risk in turn depended in part on the persuasiveness of a legal case based on Article IV and the forums in which the case might be presented. Only a decision not to act at all would have eliminated any danger of a Turkish military response. But compared to a decision to abrogate, a decision to propose revisions in the Constitution was certain to produce both a milder Turkish response and substantially less international support for Turkish use of force. The gamble involved in a decision to demand revisions of all the 1960 Accords would have been more dangerous. The Treaties of Alliance, Establishment, and Guarantee were all international agreements; the Constitution was not. True, those agreements bound the Cypriot Government not to amend the Basic Articles of the Constitution. But the argument that every state must have the right to alter the charter governing its internal affairs is substantially more powerful than contentions favouring unilateral revision of treaties. The treaties could be taken up later—and separately, except, of course, for the provisions calling for maintenance of the 'unamendable' (basic) articles in the Constitution.

B. PRESSURES FROM GREECE

In the 1950s the Greek Government had been the sole spokesman in international forums on behalf of Greek Cypriots, and was

[25] General Grivas has said that the Archbishop wrote at the time the 1960 Accords were negotiated that 'he was pleased with the agreement on the whole'. *Memoirs of General Grivas* 189 (Foley (ed.), 1965). But the General was so embittered at what he considered an unsatisfactory compromise that his account may have to be discounted.

the major force behind the drive to terminate British sovereignty over Cyprus. In 1963, of course, the Cypriot Government itself was represented in the United Nations and other international arenas. But the ethnic ties that bound Greeks and Greek Cypriots were still strong, and the Greek Government was under substantial domestic pressure to back the Archbishop on any given issue.

As in discussing the role of the Turkish Government, identification of probable Greek reactions to alternative decisions by Archbishop Makarios is easier than measuring the impact of those reactions; lack of published materials make both undertakings hazardous. With that caveat, however, speculation is possible. The starting point is the position of Greece as a primary architect of the 1960 Accords and a Guarantor Party under the Treaty of Guarantee. That agreement imposed an obligation on Greece, as well as Turkey and the United Kingdom, to maintain the arrangements negotiated at Zurich and London. Unlike the Turkish Government, the Greek Government posed no danger of unilateral armed intervention to Archbishop Makarios. But the 1960 Accords not only granted the right 'to take action with the sole aim of re-establishing the state of affairs created by the present Treaty', they also imposed an obligation to maintain the *status quo*. And the 'state of affairs created by the present Treaty' was quite different—in time and circumstances—from that established by the Treaty of Lausanne. In the 1950s, the agreement by which Greece acknowledged British rule over the Island had been negotiated three decades before as part of a World War I settlement. In 1963, the Accords that granted independence to Cyprus were only three years old and were the result of an extended diplomatic campaign by Greece toward precisely that goal. All these forces must have made Greek Government support for abrogation of the 1960 Accords seem most unlikely. The Soviet Government could be expected to urge that the Agreements were 'forced' on Cyprus—as in fact its United Nations ambassador did urge[26]—but not the Greek Government, lest Greece be labelled as a principal 'forcer'. Indeed, there is evidence that Greek representatives at the 1959 London Conference told Archbishop Makarios that if he did not accept the settlement they would wash their hands of the whole problem.[27] These

---

[26] 19 U.N. SCOR, 1096th meeting 3 (1964).
[27] Stephens, *Cyprus: A Place of Arms* 165 (1968).

pressures indicate counsel by the Greek Government not to see termination of the 1960 Accords but rather renegotiation and revision, particularly of the Constitution.

The case for revision could not be rooted in classic precepts of international law. As we saw in Chapter II, the traditional view is that, 'As a question of law, there is not much to be said upon the revision of treaties.'[28] The only well-recognized doctrine of direct relevance deals not with modification of treaties but with their termination: *rebus sic stantibus*. And whether under the so-called subjective or objective approach—or some alternative formulation—no persuasive argument could be made for its application in this context. The only change in circumstances between 1960 and 1963 was that the Accords had been tried for three years and found wanting by at least the Greek Cypriots. Their defects from the Greek Cypriot perspective could be characterized as 'fundamental'; but this would not, in the traditional view, provide an option to terminate.[29]

At the same time, it was plain in 1963 that a majority of Greek Cypriots thought that the Accords were unfair and that there would be sufficient support for their view in the international community to preclude a defence resting solely on the sanctity of treaties. Further, a persuasive case can be made that *perpetual* restrictions on the constitutional system of the Cypriot Republic, agreed to in exchange for the grant of independence, *ought* to be subject to revision, even though the agreements in which they are embodied do not provide for modification or renegotiation.[30] It is this normative judgement that could have been urged on Archbishop Makarios by Greek Government officials. It could have been bolstered by appropriate references to the 'sovereign equality' of United Nations members, and to like principles.

[28] McNair, *The Law of Treaties* 534 (1961).

[29] See generally, McNair, *Law of Treaties*, ch. 42 (1961). The Convention on the Law of Treaties, Art. 62, provides that 'a fundamental change of circumstances' may not be invoked as a ground for terminating a treaty unless 'the existence of those circumstances constituted an essential basis of the consent of the parties to be bound by the treaty' and 'the effect of the change is radically to transform the extent of obligations still to be performed under the treaty'. U.N. Doc. A/Conf. 39/27 (1969).

[30] Lester, 'Bizerta and the Unequal Treaty Theory', 11 Int'l & Comp. L.Q. 847, 855 (1962), suggests that agreements between 'dominant States and their dependent territories . . . in which the dependent agreed to onerous restrictions upon its future sovereignty in exchange for the grant of independence by the dominant State, might raise the presumption of undue influence'.

But advocates of this position must have been conscious not only of the fragile nature of the principles involved but also of the primitive state of the institutional arrangments for the renegotiation and revision of treaties. A variety of mechanisms might have been suggested, but none bears much resemblance to the international legal process as it actually operates.

Even though it could not reasonably have been expected in the fall and winter of 1963 that Turkey and the Turkish Cypriots could be quickly forced to renegotiate the Accords through the United Nations, none the less Greece probably urged the Archbishop to propose revisions of the Constitution and, if the revisions were rejected, as must have seemed likely, to take the matter to the United Nations. Several clusters of related reasons made that organization the most appropriate international institution to further Greek Cypriot interests. First, Cyprus could count on backing in the United Nations from both the Soviet bloc and many developing countries. To the Soviet Union, the crisis offered a prime opportunity publicly to attack the 1960 Accords as an unfair settlement imposed by NATO members, and thus to attack NATO itself. Further, it was certain that the Cyprus issue would again divide the NATO members, just as it had in the 1950s. To the developing countries, particularly those in the Arab bloc, Cyprus had been a leading spokesman and advocate. In these circumstances, the United Nations must have appeared as a reasonably hospitable forum in which to gain international support for revising the 1960 Accords. An added benefit would be that the Turkish Cypriots would not be represented in the United Nations, except through an intermediary—Turkey—much as Greece represented the Greek Cypriots in the 1950s.

A second advantage of bringing the problem to the United Nations was that this tactic would, as a practical matter, preclude alternative measures in the two other international arrangements that might otherwise take jurisdiction over the matter—NATO and the trio of Guarantor Powers acting under the Treaty of Guarantee. Cyprus was not a member of these institutional arrangements, and in neither one could it or even Greece expect the same favourable treatment as in the hands of the United Nations. In both institutions, the position of Turkey and the United Kingdom would be substantially stronger.

Finally, and perhaps most importantly, the United Nations

was the most obvious forum in which to check military intervention under the Treaty of Guarantee. It might be possible to gain a Security Council resolution precluding armed action by a guarantor power as in violation of the United Nations Charter. At the least, it would be possible to argue that any right to take such action was suspended while the United Nations was seized of the matter.

C. PRESSURES FROM THE UNITED KINGDOM

No published accounts are available of discussions between Greek Cypriot and British officials in the period preceding Archbishop Makarios's announcement of thirteen proposed constitutional revisions. But there certainly were consultations between the two Governments—Cyprus was and remains a member of the Commonwealth. Although analysis of the British position must be speculative, the general lines of that position seem clear enough. Again, the focus here is less on what was actually expressed by the British Government than on Archbishop Makarios's prediction of British reactions to the alternative decisions. Within that framework, the British Government was probably seen from Nicosia as just about where it was at the end of 1957: somewhere in the middle between Greece and Turkey, but with an instinct for maintaining the *status quo*.

The primary British interests were strategic—generally, to protect a unified NATO and, specifically, to protect the two British base-areas on the Island. The United Kingdom could be counted on to oppose any Cypriot effort to abrogate the Treaty of Establishment, which recognized British sovereignty over those bases. It would have been hard to formulate an argument that the entire 1960 settlement was invalid without including that treaty. Cyprus had little chance to overcome British opposition to a unilateral threat to the base-areas, particularly because of the support Britain would receive from the United States and other NATO allies.

More generally, England—like Turkey—had an obligation to help maintain the settlement negotiated in 1960 as well as a right 'to take action with the sole aim of re-establishing the state of affairs created by the present Treaty [of Guarantee]' if consultations with the other Guarantor Powers failed. Such consultations were probably viewed as the most likely first British step in response to any Cypriot move away from the 1960 Accords. If those consultations failed, a British effort to join with Turkey in settling the matter militarily must have been seen as one possibility. If the two nations moved promptly and decisively with their forces already on the Island, reinforced by troops from other bases, there was some chance that they might compel the Archbishop to back away from his goal of fundamentally restructuring the arrangements established in 1960. Greece could be counted on not to co-operate with Great Britain in a military operation on the Island, but Turkey was certain to join that operation. And there would be little danger of a military response by Greece, in contrast to the probable Greek reaction to unilateral Turkish intervention.

The Archbishop could reasonably expect international pressures against such a move by England, particularly if the matter were taken before the United Nations. Military intervention would have occasioned a good deal of anti-colonial verbal abuse against a country particularly sensitive on that subject. More serious, strong Soviet opposition to such a move would have been certain. It might even have been denounced by the United States, and the British could not forget the aftermath of their Suez intervention. Furthermore, the last years of Great Britain's rule on the Island had been bloody, as we have seen, and British leaders could have little desire to go another round. These factors could have been expected to reduce the likelihood of the British use of force. The chance could be further reduced if Cyprus took the crisis to the United Nations. In that circumstance, Cyprus and Greece might both claim that United Nations involvement had pre-empted any authority of the Guarantor Powers to use force under the Treaty of Guarantee, even assuming the Treaty sanctioned military means.

As an alternative to action under the Treaty of Guarantee, the United Kingdom might also be expected to seek resolution of the dispute within NATO. That course would have had the advantage that both Turkey and Greece were committed to NATO, and—under the procedure adopted in 1956—to peaceful resolution within the organization of any inter-NATO dispute. The organization itself had two principal interests in settling the controversy. First, the potential of armed conflict between member-states strained the Atlantic Alliance much as it had done in the 1950s. The problem weakened the entire right flank of NATO defences. Second, the organization had a strategic interest in the

Island itself, both because of the British bases there and because of the price that the Soviet Union might exact in return for supporting the Archbishop.

D THE GREEK CYPRIOT DECISION

The analysis to this point has suggested that Archbishop Makarios proposed revisions of the Constitution, rather than abrogation of all the 1960 Accords, because the Greek Cypriot claim of domestic jurisdiction was strongest regarding the Constitution, and the call for revision avoided substantial questions about the validity of unilateral abrogation. Bringing the matter to the Security Council offered the immediate opportunity to check the possibility that Turkey would intervene militarily to enforce those provisions. Over time, the Archbishop could also hope to build up international support for revising all the Accords. In the interim, most of the proposed constitutional revisions could be put into effect on a temporary basis. That is precisely the course followed by the Cypriot Government.

Whether or not the Archbishop viewed his decision to propose thirteen constitutional revisions as a step toward the effective abrogation of the 1960 Accords, the choice of revision rather than termination had an important impact on subsequent events. The Archbishop was obviously not able to control those events completely. But he was largely successful in limiting the ability of other nations to control it. A major share of that success was due to the way in which he framed his decision.

On 25 December 1963, the Turkish Foreign Minister was reported to have announced that 'Turkey decided to use her own right of unilateral intervention on the basis of article IV of the Treaty of Guarantee, but she confined her intervention to a single warning flight of jet fighters of the Turkish air force . . .'[31] In response, a Security Council meeting was held on 27 December to consider Cypriot charges that Turkey had committed 'acts of (a) aggression, (b) intervention in the internal affairs of Cyprus by the threat and use of force against its territorial integrity . . .'[32] No specific proposals for United Nations measures were made by any Council members. But the organization had arguably be-

[31] 19 U.N. SCOR, 1098th meeting 15–16 (1964).
[32] See Letter From the Permanent Representative of Cyprus to the President of the Security Council, 26 Dec. 1963, in U.N. Doc. No. S/5488, at 1 (1963); 18 U.N. SCOR, 1085th meeting (1963).

come seized of the crisis; this was a critical element in the Archbishop's ability to check the efforts of other nations to resolve the dispute outside the United Nations.

On Christmas Day, when it was apparent that violence was increasing throughout Cyprus, the three Guarantor Powers informed the Cypriot Government 'of their readiness to assist if invited to do so, in restoring peace and order by means of a joint peace-making force under British command' and composed of British, Greek, and Turkish contingents already present on the Island under the Treaties of Establishment and Alliance.[33] In the British view, the Guarantor Powers would be acting as a 'regional arrangement' established under the Treaty of Guarantee and authorized by Chapter VIII of the United Nations Charter.[34] During the House of Commons debate on the matter, the British Minister of State was pressed to 'give an assurance that the proposed force will not be sent until the authorization by the Security Council is received'. The Minister refused, claiming that 'this question is purely hypothetical'.[35] The Cypriot Government agreed to a temporary ceasefire under the supervision of the Guarantor Powers while those powers and the two communities on the Island sought to resolve their differences at another London conference. But the Archbishop insisted that the four Governments jointly request the United Nations Secretary-General to appoint a representative 'to observe the progress of the peace-making operation'.[36] At a London meeting it soon became clear that the differences among the parties were too deep for easy resolution. The Archbishop maintained that he was seeking no more than a reasonable way to enable the machinery of Cypriot Government to function—and that meant altering the 1960 settlement to allow government by the Greek majority with

[33] See U.N. Doc. No. S/5508, at 2 (1964).

[34] See 688 H.C. Deb. (5th ser.) 530–1 (1964).

[35] Id. at 815–17. A year before, United States representatives had contended that the quarantine of Cuba was not 'enforcement action' by a regional arrangement within the meaning of Article 53. See Meeker, 'Defensive Quarantine and the Law', 57 Am. J. Int'l L. 515, 520–2 (1963). They also maintained that even if the quarantine had been 'enforcement action', it would not have been precluded by Article 53 since the Security Council 'authorization' required by that provision need be neither 'prior' nor 'express'. See ibid. The British Government may have been concerned that a direct response to the question referred to above would have cast doubt on the United States legal position in the Cuban crisis.

[36] U.N. Doc. No. S/5508, at 3 (1964).

constitutional guarantees of Turkish Cypriot civil. rights. But Turkey and the Turkish Cypriots would not accept such a scheme. In these circumstances, the Archbishop insisted that the United Nations was the only international forum in which the crisis could be resolved.

The Archbishop followed a similar line when the British Government next developed a plan with the United States for an enlarged peacekeeping force drawn from NATO nations.[37] It was never wholly clear whether and to what extent this force would have been responsible to the Cypriot Government, to the Guarantor Powers, to the other countries supplying contingents, or to NATO. Although Greece and Turkey supported the plan, it appeared from the outset as an Anglo-American scheme.[38] Few other European governments wished to become involved, and, at least in retrospect, there would seem to have been little chance of acceptance by Archbishop Makarios. He wanted to take his case to the United Nations where, as soon became clear, he hoped to gain the organization's condemnation of the 1960 Accords. To this end he carefully sought to maintain his position as leader of a non-aligned nation. And he gained strong support from the Soviet Union, which repeatedly warned the NATO powers to stay out of the internal affairs of Cyprus.[39] An attempt was made to make the proposal more palatable to the Cypriot Government by stipulating that the Guarantor Powers would not 'exercise their rights of unilateral intervention under article IV of the Treaty of Guarantee' for a three-month period while a

[37] Duncan Sandys, Secretary of State for Commonwealth Relations and for the Colonies, offered two reasons for inviting 'certain other members of the NATO Alliance to provide the necessary troops, though not, of course, as a NATO operation or under NATO control . . . The first was that these countries had forces close at hand and immediately available. The second was that all NATO members had a direct interest in stopping an inter-communal conflict in Cyprus which, if allowed to develop, could all too easily lead to a clash between two NATO allies.' 689 H.C. Deb. (5th ser.) 841 (1964). The British representative to the Security Council did not, however, even mention NATO in describing the plan to the Council, but referred instead to 'an enlarged peace-keeping force drawn from countries friendly to Cyprus'. See 19 U.N. SCOR, 1095th meeting 10 (1964).

[38] See Windsor, *NATO and the Cyprus Crisis*. Adelphi Paper No. 14, Nov. 1964, p. 13.

[39] See, e.g., Letter from the U.N. Representative of the U.S.S.R. to the President of the Security Council, 8 Feb. 1964, in U.N. Doc. No. S/5534 (1964).

solution was being negotiated with the assistance of a mutually acceptable mediator.[40] In spite of this sweetener, the Archbishop lost no time in rejecting the plan. He concurred —or at least acquiesced—in the stationing of an international force on the Island, but insisted that it be under the Security Council, that it not include Greek or Turkish troops, and that its mandate include protection of the territorial integrity of Cyprus and assistance in restoring normal conditions.[41] When these efforts to resolve the crisis outside the United Nations failed, it was brought directly to the Security Council. It is difficult to determine whether the Archbishop considered that one consequence of proposing constitutional revisions might be to give Cyprus a semipermanent place on the United Nation agenda. In all events, the problem has been there ever since.

[40] 19 U.N. SCOR, 1095th meeting 10 (1964).
[41] Id. at 10–11.

IV

THE
TURKISH GOVERNMENT'S DECISION
IN 1964 TO BOMB CYPRUS

ON 7 and 8 August 1964, Turkish air force planes bombed Greek Cypriot troops who were attacking a Turkish Cypriot enclave on the Island's north-west coast. The attacks caused substantial loss of life to many unarmed civilians as well as to Greek Cypriot soldiers. A ceasefire was negotiated on 9 August after intense pressures both within and without the United Nations. This Chapter examines how law affected both the Turkish decision to use force and the ways in which that force was used.

The decision came against a background of some six months of active United Nations involvement in the crisis. On 15 February 1964, the British and Cypriot representatives to the United Nations separately requested the Security Council to consider ways to resolve the crisis that had already brought almost two months of bloodshed to the Island.[1] After many days of negotiation, the Council worked out a resolution acceptable to all sides; it was adopted on 4 March.[2] The resolution noted that 'the present situation with regard to Cyprus is likely to threaten international peace and security'. It called upon all members 'to refrain from any action or threat of action likely to worsen the situation in the sovereign Republic of Cyprus' and upon 'the communities in Cyprus and their leaders to act with utmost restraint'. The resolution also recommended the creation, 'with the consent of the Government of Cyprus', of a United Nations peacekeeping force in Cyprus.

The United Nations force became operational at the end of March 1964, and reached its planned level of about 7,000 men in May. The troops tried, with a fair degree of success, to prevent incidents from becoming full-fledged fights, generally by attempt-

---

[1] See U.N. Docs. No. S/5543, S/5544 (1964).
[2] U.N. Doc. No. S/5575 (1964).

ing to interpose between the two factions and talking to each side's local leader. But tension on the Island was never far below the boiling point. In June 1964, Archbishop Makarios announced the introduction of military conscription—presumably of only Greek Cypriots and, of course, without concurrence of the Turkish representatives in the government. Late that month, General Grivas returned to Cyprus to train the new Cyprus National Guard. Soldiers and arms began to pour into Cyprus, mostly from Greece but also some from Turkey.

The Cypriot Government, with Turkish representatives now gone, undertook in July a series of legislative and judicial reforms designed to consolidate its control. The Government also tried to isolate the Turkish-held areas from the rest of the Island. It stopped fuel trucks and other supplies that might be used for military purposes, and restricted shipments from the Turkish Red Crescent. Some 20,000 Turkish Cypriots had left, or were forced from, their homes soon after the crisis began. Turkish leaders claimed that these displaced persons would be subject to further attacks if they returned to their homes.[3] The Cypriot Government alleged that these reports were unfounded and charged Turkey with encouraging the refugees to remain in armed camps, protected by Turkish Cypriot forces, to preserve the position that partition or federation are the only possible solutions to the crisis.[4] Wherever the truth lies, and there may be some on both sides, the Cypriot Government unquestionably maintained a virtual economic blockade against these camps during much of the crisis.

Then at the beginning of August, a Cypriot Government force launched a series of attacks against the Kokkina–Mansoura area on the north-western coast, one of the last stretches of seashore held by Turkish Cypriots. Turkish Cypriots had been leaving their homes in the north-western section of the Island to concentrate in the area; as time went on, they could be expected to strengthen their defences. The area was allegedly a main landing spot for arms and other supplies from Turkey. The Cypriot Government also claimed that it was a centre of terrorists who

[3] See 20 U.N. SCOR 1235th meeting 17 (1965) (statement of Mr. Rauf Denktash, President of the Turkish Cypriot Communal Chamber).

[4] See, e.g., Public Information Office, Republic of Cyprus, 'The Turkish Cypriot Refugees' Plight: Human Misery Used to Further Political Aims', in *Cyprus Bull.*, 16 Oct. 1965, p. 4.

'were carrying out a plan . . . to spread and intensify the rebellion in Cyprus, and resort to warfare and everything that goes
with warfare . . .'[5] The Turkish Government responded that the
Archbishop intended 'to wipe out the inhabitants of the
area . . .'[6]

Until August, food, clothing, and other supplies for the inhabitants of the area had been brought from Turkey by ship and
landed on the coast. But now the threat was military, not just
economic. The United Nations force had a unit in the area, and
the Greek Cypriot attacks violated an express assurance given by
Archbishop Makarios to the United Nations force commander.[7]
When fighting between troops of the two factions began, the
force commander tried to negotiate a ceasefire. The United Nations force also made an unsuccessful effort to evacuate women
and children from the area. When words failed, however, the
United Nations unit withdrew, rather than get involved in the
combat itself. Presumably sometime during 6 August the Turkish
Government made the final decision to send its jet-fighters to
attack the Greek Cypriot forces.

The Turkish Government was under substantial domestic
pressures to aid the Turkish Cypriots. In early December 1963,
Inonu had resigned as prime minister when the opposition Justice
Party showed sharp gains in a local election. The Christmas Day
crisis brought him back to power—in part because he was seen as
one who could deal effectively with the Cyprus situation. Further,
his coalition government depended in some degree on support
from the leaders of the armed forces. Those leaders were presumably pressing Inonu to adopt a military 'solution' from the outset
of the crisis. The Turkish armed services, about 500,000 men,
were about three times as large as the Greek forces, and the
Turkish air force was comparably superior.[8]

August 1964 was not the first occasion during the crisis when
the Turkish use of force was at issue. As we have seen, 'a warning
flight' of Turkish jet-fighters was sent over the Island on Christmas Day 1963. On 12 March 1964, Turkey threatened to invade

[5] 19 U.N. SCOR, 1142d meeting 18 (1964).

[6] Id. at 10.

[7] See Secretary-General, Report on the United Nations Operations in
Cyprus, U.N. Doc. No. S/5950, at 23 (1964).

[8] See *N.Y. Times*, 10 Aug. 1964, p. 12, col. 8. The precise military figures are
classified. See Hearings on the Foreign Assistance Act of 1964 Before the House
Committee on Foreign Affairs, 88th Cong., 2d Sess., pt. IV, at 522–3 (1964).

Cyprus unless 'all . . . assaults . . . against the Turkish Community in Cyprus . . . [are] stopped . . . [and] an immediate cease-fire . . . [is] established . . .' [9] Turkey backed away from this threat, but only under strong Security Council pressure.[10] In June 1964, the Turkish Government came to the brink of deciding to occupy a portion of the Island by force. Again it was dissuaded; this time by an urgent appeal from President Johnson.[11] Mr. Inonu survived an Assembly vote of confidence in June by a vote of only 200 to 194.[12]

Each time that Turkey threatened to use force, but did not carry out its threat, the likelihood that it would ever actually intervene seemed to lessen. As the credibility of Turkish armed action diminished, the danger increased that the Cypriot Government would make an effort to resolve the Island's troubles by force. But major obstacles to that effort were posed by Turkey's supply of military equipment and the threat of Turkish intervention. The Greek Cypriot offensive in early August may have appeared to Turkish leaders as the first step in an intensive campaign to remove at least the major pockets of Turkish Cypriot resistance. The Kokkina–Mansoura area was one of the most important of those pockets.

Law was obviously not the sole determinant of Turkey's decision to use force or how to use it. Turkish representatives must also have weighed, for example, the risk that an attack on Cyprus would trigger a Soviet military response against Turkey. But a primary concern of the Turkish Government was the extent to which it could appeal for international support or at least preclude international censure, perhaps even sanctions. A sound legal case was a necessary component of those efforts.

In considering possible military action against Cyprus, Turkish

[9] See Letter From the Permanent Representative of Turkey to the Secretary-General, 13 Mar. 1964, in U.N. Doc. No. S/5596, Annex, at 2 (1964). Turkey also demanded that 'all sieges around any Turkish locality be lifted forthwith anywhere; the liberties of complete movement, communication and correspondence be immediately restored and that the Turkish hostages and the bodies of those murdered be returned to the Turkish Community without delay'. Ibid.

[10] See 19 U.N. SCOR, 1103d meeting (1964), and the resolution that resulted from that meeting, U.N. Doc. No. S/5603 (1964).

[11] See the letter to Prime Minister Inonu from President Johnson, dated 5 June 1964, reprinted in Public Information Office of the Republic of Cyprus, *Cyprus: The Problem in Perspective* 33-4 (1968).

[12] See Davison, *Turkey* 160 (1968).

legal advisers knew they would have to defend that action in the United Nations—certainly in the Security Council, and possibly in the General Assembly as well. The Cypriot Government had sought to make the Council a tribunal for judging Turkey's threats to use force against Cyprus. Cypriot representatives were certain to seek Council condemnation and sanctions if those threats were carried out. Until August, the posture of the dispute had been in the nature of a suit by Cyprus for a declaratory judgement that a Turkish use of force would violate the United Nations Charter. Turkey had successfully resisted that suit, in large measure by basing its argument on the importance of maintaining the 1960 treaties except with the consent of all parties and by pointing to Archbishop Makarios's efforts to force unilateral revision. The Council's resolution of 4 March called upon all United Nations members 'to refrain from any action or threat of action likely to worsen the situation in the sovereign Republic of Cyprus, or to endanger international peace'. But it contained no explicit prohibition against Turkish military intervention. But if Turkey actually used force—as opposed to merely threatening its use—the stakes would be much higher before the Council; only a persuasive case could prevent a strong Council reaction. That might mean a resolution formally censuring Turkey; it might also include some among the range of sanctions authorized in Chapter VII of the Charter.

The Turkish Government defended each threat to intervene on the basis of Article IV of the Treaty of Guarantee. That article states:

In the event of a breach of the provisions of the present Treaty, Greece, Turkey and the United Kingdom undertake to consult together with respect to the representations or measures necessary to ensure observance of those provisions.

In so far as common or concerted action may not prove possible, each of the three guaranteeing Powers reserves the right to take action with the sole aim of re-establishing the state of affairs created by the present Treaty.

From the outset of the crisis, the Turkish Government had claimed that this provision authorized military intervention to protect Turkish Cypriot rights established by the 1960 settlement. The claim had been consistently resisted by the Cypriot and Greek Governments. Cyprus came to the Security Council in early 1964 with hopes of precluding such an interpretation. Cypriot representatives maintained that the use of force was neither permitted by the terms of Article IV nor consistent with the United Nations Charter. Through the spring and early summer of 1964, Turkey had been able to resist that claim. But the arguments pressed by Turkey to meet the Cypriot legal position also restricted the situations in which Turkey might intervene. Unilateral action under Article IV is limited to 're-establishing the state of affairs created by the present Treaty' and requires prior consultations with the other Guarantor Powers. The very process of legitimizing the use of force thus restrained that use.

In this situation, Turkey could continue to rely on Article IV of the Treaty of Guarantee or shift to an argument based on self-defence. Previously, Turkish representatives had not publicly claimed that a Turkish military action against Cyprus could be in self-defence. The claim might have been based either on Article 51 of the United Nations Charter or on customary international law. An obvious advantage of Article 51 would have been to avoid the question whether that provision precludes the exercise of a broader right of self-defence under customary law.[13] Further, Article 51 specifically raises above other Charter obligations the right 'of individual or collective self-defence if an armed attack occurs . . . until the Security Council has taken the measures necessary to maintain international peace and security'. In the circumstances of early August 1964, Turkey could claim that it was responding to a Cypriot armed attack. At the same time, characterization of Turkish bombing attacks against Cyprus as self-defence under Article 51 should have raised troublesome issues in the minds of Turkish legal advisers. Cyprus and Greece— and other nations as well—could be expected to charge that the Security Council had precluded unilateral action under Article 51 by taking 'measures necessary to maintain international peace and security'. Turkey would have to show that the United Nations troops had been unable to implement those measures. The fact that Greek Cypriot troops had attacked in violation of an express assurance by Archbishop Makarios to the United Nations force commander would be substantial evidence for the Turkish position. Unless the measures taken by the Security

---

[13] Compare Brownlie, *International Law and the Use of Force by States* 272–5 (1963), with Bowett, *Self-Defense in International Law* 184–93 (1958).

Council were effectively implemented, Turkey could forcefully argue that its rights under Article 51 had not been cut off. It would be more difficult to claim, however, that any 'armed attack' had been 'against a Member of the United Nations' within the meaning of Article 51.

Several other lines of argument could have been expected against a Turkish claim of self-defence, whether it was rooted in customary international law or in Article 51. One would have been that armed action was neither necessary nor proportionate to the dangers involved. Again, however, Turkey could point to the Greek Cypriot offensive as a scheme to exterminate the Turkish Cypriot population in the Kokkina–Mansoura area. Turkish representatives could claim that only a forceful response would check an otherwise certain slaughter. The persuasiveness of that argument would depend in large part on Turkey's ability to marshal evidence of what was actually happening on the Island during the critical period. Even today those facts are obscure.

Turkey could also expect to face at least a conceptual hurdle in describing a military action against Cyprus as self-defence. The use of force to protect a nation's citizens has been justified on the ground that a state is no more than a collectivity of its nationals, and, therefore, that protection of them is protection of the state itself.[14] The ties that bind Turkish Cypriots to Turkey are strong. For many they may be stronger than their bonds with the Island. And in the eyes of Turkey, their defence was undoubtedly the defence of Turkey. But many in the United Nations could be expected to question whether Turkish Cypriots should be viewed as an extension of Turkey's 'self' since they lack 'a nexus of nationality'.[15]

The alternative legal defence of Turkish military intervention in August would be based on Article IV of the Treaty of Guarantee. In order to make a persuasive case for unilateral military action under Article IV, Turkey had to show that: (1) the Cypriot Government had violated the terms of the treaty; (2) the re-

[14] See Bowett, *Self-Defense in International Law* 91–4 (1958).
[15] See id. at 95. The United States initially justified intervention in the Dominican Republic in 1965 on the ground that it 'was essential to preserve the lives of foreign nationals—nationals of the United States *and of many other countries*'. Legal Adviser, U.S. Dep't of State, Legal Basis for United States Actions in the Dominican Republic, 7 May 1965.

quired consultation among the Guarantor Powers had occurred;
(3) 'common or concerted action' had not proved possible; (4)
the right to take 'action' included the right to use force; and (5)
the use of force 'to re-establish the state of affairs' created by the
treaty was consistent with Turkey's obligations under the United
Nations Charter.

In the view of Turkey and the Turkish Cypriots, the first pre-
condition to armed 'action' against Cyprus had been met in the
spring of 1964. Article I of the Treaty of Guarantee required
Cyprus to 'undertake to ensure . . . respect for its Constitution'.
At the very least, this implies a substantial good-faith effort to
make the Constitution work. Turkey could cite considerable
evidence that the efforts of Archbishop Makarios were inadequate. He claimed Turkish Cypriot 'abuses' of the Constitution
as his justification.[16] But Turkey could properly respond that
even assuming such abuses, they did not support, for example,
the Cypriot Government's refusal to implement a number of
basic articles of the Constitution, such as the one requiring
separate Turkish Cypriot municipalities in each of Cyprus's four
largest towns.

Turkey could also defend the claim that the second and third
conditions precedent to unilateral action by one of the Guarantor
Powers had been met. As we have seen, British, Greek, and Turkish officials conferred with representatives of the Cypriot communities in January 1964 'to help in the solution of the problem
of Cyprus'.[17] As an interim measure, troops of the three Guarantor Powers, under British command, had sought to preserve a
ceasefire and to restore peace. Both efforts failed. Those failures
cannot be ascribed to Greek Cypriot intransigency alone, but
that was a primary factor. After the conference reached a dead-
lock, the British had proposed a NATO peacekeeping force, and
Greece as well as Turkey had concurred. But the Archbishop
rejected the proposal.

The fourth requirement in Article IV raised more difficult
problems. The Cypriot Government had taken the position that
the term 'action' in Article IV—like 'measures' in the preceding
clauses—'could only mean the use of peaceful means . . .'[18] None
of the Guarantor Powers brought to light any negotiation history

[16] See *The Times* (London) 5 Jan. 1962, p. 10, col. 5.
[17] U.N. Doc. No. S/5508, at 3 (1964).
[18] 19 U.N. SCOR, 1098th meeting 19 (1964).

concerning Article IV,[19] though the Greek representative stated
that '[a]t Zurich, where I was present, our intention was not to
create a situation in which, for one reason or another, one of us
might be able, one fine day, to put troops on our warships and
dispatch them to Cyprus.'[20] It is at least possible that the parties
simply could not agree on the scope of permissible action and,
therefore, consciously accepted ambiguity with the hope that the
issue would never arise. And it could be argued that the ambiguity
should be interpreted against those who would impose a limitation on Cypriot sovereignty.[21]

Turkey could persuasively claim, however, that the circumstances in which the Treaty of Guarantee was negotiated make it
seem probable that the Guarantor Powers contemplated use of
force as a possible action under Article IV. As we have seen, the
Zurich–London settlement was reached at a time of bloodshed
and violence on the Island. The constitutional guarantees of the
Turkish minority were intended to stabilize the situation. But if
these guarantees failed, the parties were entitled to intervene to
restore the 'state of affairs created by the Treaty'. In light of the
Island's history of strife, it seems unlikely that the parties believed diplomatic protests and economic sanctions would in all
cases be adequate. The stationing of Greek and Turkish military
forces on Cyprus under the Treaty of Alliance—when viewed
together with the Treaty of Establishment, which provides for
sovereign British bases on the Island—provides some support for

---

[19] Apparently the *travaux préparatoires* of the Zurich and London Conferences have been sealed to outside inspection. See Blümel, 'Die Verfassungs-
gerichtsbarkeit in der Republik Zypern', in *Constitutional Review in the World
Today* 643, 652 n. 49 (Max-Planck-Instit. 1962). No evidence was produced to
indicate that the parties were using the terms 'action' and 'measures' in the
same sense they are used in the United Nations Charter; the fact that the
Expenses case involved the meaning of both words seems more coincidental
than revealing. See *Certain Expenses of the United Nations*, [1962] I.C.J. 151,
162–5.

[20] 19 U.N. SCOR, 1097th meeting 32 (1964).

[21] See McNair, *The Law of Treaties* 462–3 (1961). The principle that ambiguous treaty provisions should be interpreted against the drafting party might also
have been advanced by Cyprus. See id. at 464–5. Apparently, neither rule of
interpretation has been voiced by the Cypriot Government. It has, however,
maintained that military intervention would conflict with Articles 2(4) and
2(1) of the United Nations Charter, as discussed below, and that Article IV of
the Treaty of Guarantee should, therefore, be interpreted to exclude such
intervention. See 19 U.N. SCOR, 1098th meeting 17 (1964).

this view. If troops were needed on the Island by any of the Guarantor Powers, they would already be present.

Assuming that Turkey could meet these first four hurdles toward a showing that its unilateral use of force under Article IV was justified, it would still have to show the consistency of that action with the United Nations Charter. It was on the cluster of issues concerning this question that the Cypriot Government, supported by Greece, could be expected to raise the strongest legal claims.

A. PRESSURES FROM THE GOVERNMENTS OF CYPRUS AND GREECE

The Government of Archbishop Makarios wanted to exert every possible influence on Turkey not to intervene militarily. We have seen that this interest was one of the main motivations behind the Archbishop's insistence that the United Nations be the only international arrangement directly involved in maintaining peace on the Island and in seeking to resolve the crisis. As in the past, Greece could be counted on to support the general Cypriot approach. On the issue of Turkish military intervention, Greek backing for Cyprus was assured. However troublesome the Archbishop had been to the Greek Government on occasions, a Turkish attack would inevitably occasion enormous pressures within Greece for a military response. But Turkey had a substantial military advantage over Greece. The Turkish population was more than triple the size of the Greek population, and the Turkish armed forces were about three times as large as the Greek forces. Greek officials had no interest in being drawn into any conflict, particularly when the odds would have been so heavily against them.

Article IV of the Treaty of Guarantee was a focal point in the general Cypriot campaign in the Security Council. Again and again, Cyprus tried to gain support for the position that Turkey was precluded from military intervention under Article IV. It pressed a two-pronged argument: first, that the Treaty did not authorize the use of force; second, if force was sanctioned by the Treaty, it was void *ab initio* as inconsistent with the United Nations Charter. At the first Council meeting concerning the dispute, the Cypriot representative, Mr. Rossides, took the offensive by claiming that a Turkish invasion fleet had been steaming toward the Island.[22] The facts of the matter—whether

[22] 18 U.N. SCOR, 1085th meeting 3 (1963).

there was any such fleet, and if so whether it was being used as a threat or with the real intention of landing a military force—have never been made clear. The Turkish representative, Mr. Kural, declaimed with some passion that Cyprus was merely crying wolf to avoid focusing Council attention on the real issue—mistreatment of Turkish Cypriots.[23] Whatever the facts, Mr. Rossides did succeed in making the issue of Turkey's rights under Article IV a main focus of Council debate. He sought to act as both public prosecutor and plaintiff, and to position Mr. Kural as defendant before a tribunal whose role was to judge the interpretation and validity of an international agreement.

A Security Council resolution declaring that Turkey had no right to use force under Article IV of the Treaty of Guarantee would have served two Cypriot purposes. First, it would have lessened the risk of Turkish military action against the Island. The Cypriots were obviously deeply concerned about this threat —and with some justification, for the Island had no defences against a Turkish air attack. Second, such a resolution would have been a major step in gaining international concurrence, or at least acquiescence, in Cypriot renunciation of the Treaty of Guarantee and perhaps the other 1960 Agreements as well.

'Since this point has been made relevant to the whole issue,' Mr. Kyprianou said during one debate,

I should like, with permission, to put a simple question to the Members signatories to the Treaty of Guarantee . . . Is it the view of the Governments of Greece, Turkey and the United Kingdom that they have the right of military intervention under the Treaty of Guarantee, particularly, in view of the Charter? On this I must insist upon having an answer.[24]

Only the Greek representative gave an unequivocal answer. 'Do we—the Greek Government—think that this article gives us the right to intervene militarily and unilaterally without the authorization of the Security Council? The answer is "no".'[25]

The Turkish representative refused to respond directly.[26] This reluctance to meet the question squarely was undoubtedly due in part to concern that Cyprus might have gained a Security

[23] Id. at 11–12.
[24] 19 U.N. SCOR, 1097th meeting 28 (1964).
[25] Id. at 32.
[26] 19 U.N. SCOR, 1097th meeting 30 (1964).

Council resolution favouring her position if the issue had been brought to a vote. In any event, there was little chance that the Council would voice a consensus in support of Turkish military intervention. It was to Turkey's advantage, therefore, to avoid a showdown on the issue, just as it was to the advantage of Cyprus to force one. Beyond these considerations, Turkey wanted as a tactical matter to become plaintiff and prosecutor, forcing Cyprus into the position of defendant. Several times, therefore, the Turkish representative repeated this theme: Greece 'has attempted to put us in the position of the accused. We are the "aggressors". We are the ones who "threaten". We are not; we are the ones who accuse. The facts are there to be seen and, as I have said, no eloquence can change them.'[27] He tried to change the issue to whether the Cypriot representative 'can . . . solemnly and officially declare that Turkish houses will not be burned down; that Turkish Cypriot villages will not be surrounded and left without water, food and light; . . . that an end will be put to bloodshed.'[28] But debate still focused on Article IV.

In the event of an actual Turkish attack on Cyprus, Turkish representatives knew they would either have to answer 'yes' to Mr. Kyprianou's question or rely on a claim of self-defence. Presumably they would have preferred to continue relying on the Treaty of Guarantee. But as Cypriot and Greek officials had frequently argued, that position raised a number of serious issues in terms of the Charter. Cyprus, Greece, the Soviet Union, and no doubt other nations could be expected to press those issues vigorously in the event of a Turkish attack.

Cyprus and Greece had frequently claimed that Turkish military intervention would violate both the 'sovereign equality' accorded Cyprus under Article 2(1) of the Charter and the prohibition against the 'use of force' contained in Article 2(4).[29] On this basis, they claimed that Article IV of the Treaty of Guarantee, to the extent it authorized forcible action, was void under Article 103 of the Charter.[30]

[27] 19 U.N. SCOR, 1103d meeting 13 (1964).   [28] Id., p. 13.

[29] e.g. 19 U.N. SCOR, 1098th meeting 16–17 (1964).

[30] Article 103 may be read as restricted to cases in which the conflicting obligations are those of a single country. Thus, for example, a nation's Charter obligations to impose economic sanctions against another state might be inconsistent with its treaty obligations to trade with that state. Under such an interpretation, Article 103 could not be applicable in the Cyprus situation, since the alleged conflict is between the Turkish obligations under Charter

Turkey could point out, however, that there was no international consensus concerning the implications of sovereign equality.[31] A number of states have contended that there is considerable substantive content in the provision, although they have not

Articles 2(1) and 2(4) and the Cypriot obligations to respect Turkey's rights under the Treaty of Guarantee. But this seems an unnecessarily restrictive reading of Article 103 in light of its apparent purpose—to assure the primacy of the Charter.

Neither the Security Council nor the General Assembly has ever declared a treaty void under Article 103, although the issue has been raised in both bodies. See, e.g., 1 U.N. SCOR, 22d meeting 318–19 (1946) (Anglo-French Agreement of 1945); 7 U.N. GAOR, 1st Comm. 257 (1952) (Franco-Tunisian treaties of 1881 and 1883). During the General Assembly consideration of the Franco-Tunisian treaties the Australian representative contended that Article 103 'gave no competence to the United Nations and merely stated that the Charter should prevail over agreements . . .' 7 U.N. GAOR, 1st Comm. 258 (1952). The Indian representative, however, urged that the United Nations could at least 'call the attention of the Member State to that divergence . . .' 8 U.N. GAOR, 1st Comm. 39 (1953).

The Charter drafters expressly rejected a provision that would have required states, upon admission to the organization, to procure their release from treaties that were inconsistent with the Charter. See Doc. No. 934, IV/2/43, 13 U.N. Conf. Int'l Org. Docs. 701, 706–8 (1945). Such a provision was contained in Article 20(2) of the Covenant of the League of Nations and, if it had been adopted at San Francisco, might have provided a basis for asserting that a nation must either allege at the time of its admission to the United Nations a conflict between the Charter and a treaty or be thereafter held to accept their consistency. The provision was rejected primarily on the ground that some inconsistencies might not become evident until an actual controversy arose. See ibid.; U.S. Delegation to the U.N. Conference on International Organizations, Report to the President on the Results of the San Francisco Conference 155–7 (1945).

A somewhat different argument from that suggested in the text above was also developed by Cypriot representatives who claimed that any treaty authorization of force was superseded by a peremptory norm of international law unless expressly authorized by the Charter. See Jacovides, *Treaties Conflicting with Peremptory Norms of International Law and the Zurich–London 'Agreements'* (1968).

[31] See Special Committee on Principles of International Law Concerning Friendly Relations and Co-operation Among States, Consideration of Principles of International Law, U.N. Doc. No. A/5746, at 148–70 (1964). General notions of the equality of sovereign states were developed by seventeenth- and eighteenth-century nationalists; see Dickinson, *The Equality of States in International Law* 68–99 (1920), but the Four-Power declaration at Moscow in 1943 was apparently the first occasion when the phrase 'sovereign equality' was included in an international understanding. See generally U.N. Doc. No. A/C.6/L.537, at 186–210 (1963); Baxter, *Study of the Principles of International Law Concerning Friendly Relations and Co-operation Among States in Accordance With the Charter of the United Nations*, pt. 4 (1965).

always agreed on its dimensions.[32] The San Francisco proceedings and the subsequent practice of the United Nations provide little support, however, for such a view.[33] They indicate that sovereign equality neither confers rights nor imposes obligations in addition to those created elsewhere in the Charter. Rather, it assures that those rights and obligations will be shared without discrimination by all United Nations members, except of course on the basis of differences specified in the Charter.[34]

[32] Compare the Czech and four-nation proposals in Special Committee on Principles of International Law, *supra* note 31, at 148–50.

[33] The subcommittee that drafted Article 2 defined 'sovereign equality' to mean: '(1) that states are juridically equal; (2) that each state enjoys the rights inherent in full sovereignty; (3) that the personality of the state is respected, as well as its territorial integrity and political independence; (4) that the state should, under international order, comply faithfully with its international duties and obligations.' Doc. No. 944, I/1/34 (1), 6 U.N. Conf. Int'l Org. Docs. 446, 457 (1945). The only other element of 'sovereign equality' on which the Special Committee on Principles of International Law Concerning Friendly Relations and Co-operation Among States could reach agreement during its 1964 Mexico City meeting was that 'each state has the right freely to choose and develop its political, social, economic and cultural systems'. See U.N. Doc. No. A/5746, at 163 (1964).

The doctrine of sovereign equality has been referred to expressly in a number of General Assembly resolutions, but none sheds significant light on its substance. See, e.g., U.N. General Assembly Res. No. 1004 (ES-II), U.N. GAOR 2nd Emergency Sess., Supp. No. 1, at 2 (A/3355) (1956). The principle has been invoked in debates before both the General Assembly and the Security Council, but it seems to have been employed in these instances more as a rhetorical device than as a substantive principle. A number of nations, for example, have challenged 'unjust' or 'unequal' treaties on the basis of Article 2(1). See, e.g., 18 U.N. GAOR, 6th Comm. 221–2 (1963) (statement by the Cuban representative); 2 U.N. SCOR, 175th meeting 1753–4 (1947) (statement by the Egyptian representative).

[34] See 18 U.N. GAOR, 6th Comm. 256–7 (1963) (statement by the United States representative); 7 U.N. GAOR, 1st Comm. 258 (1952) (statement by the Australian representative) ('obligations . . . should not be confused with objectives, aims or purposes which did not amount to obligations'); Broms, *The Doctrine of Equality of States as Applied in International Organizations* 162–6 (1959). For a criticism of theorists who confound 'equality before the law' with 'legal equality' see Dickinson, *supra*, note 31, at 3–5; Baker, 'The Doctrine of Legal Equality of States', Brit. Yb. Int'l L. 1, 2 (1923–4).

Some treaty restrictions may be so onerous as to make meaningless the imposition of the obligations of United Nations membership. See Higgins, *The Development of International Law Through the Political Organs of the United Nations* 31–4 (1963). Miss Higgins states that because of the military facilities on Cyprus reserved to the United Kingdom under the Treaty of Establishment, the Cypriot Republic 'would seem to come very close to the borderline of lack of true inde-

Article 2(4) raises more troublesome issues. That provision requires member-states to 'refrain in their international relations from the threat or use of force against the territorial integrity or political independence of any state, or in any other manner inconsistent with the Purposes of the United Nations'. Cyprus and Greece urged that Turkey's obligations under Article 2(4) necessarily preclude any armed action under the Treaty of Guarantee.[35]

---

pendence, yet no voice of protest was raised against the admission of Cyprus'. Id. at 34. (Footnote omitted.) The Cyprus Government, in fact, has suggested that 'since . . . the sovereignty of Cyprus is not complete but is subject to foreign intervention owing to the existence of these [the 1960] Agreements, one may reasonably argue that Cyprus should not have been accepted as a member of the U.N.' Cyprus Government Press Office, *The Roots of Evil*, 21 Feb. 1964. But the Cypriot Government has not suggested that it would withdraw from the organization on this basis, but rather has turned the issue around and declared that because it is a United Nations member the Agreements are void. And since the San Francisco Conference, the political processes by which states have been admitted to the organization belie the notion that 'sovereign equality' is a meaningful prerequisite to membership.

[35] See, e.g., 19 U.N. SCOR, 1235th meeting 63-5 (1964). See also Antonopoulos, 'Les Tendances constitutionnelles des états ayant accédé récemment à l'indépendance', 15 Revue Hellénique de Droit International 307, 316 (1962); Constantopoulos, 'The Right of Intervention', International Relations (Athens), Aug. 1964, pp. 41, 43. But see Lavroff, 'Le Statut de Chypre', 65 Revue Générale de Droit International Public 527, 543 (1961); cf. De Smith, *The New Commonwealth and Its Constitutions* 285 (1964).

Cyprus maintained that Article 37 of the International Law Commission's draft Law of Treaties supported its position. That Article provided that 'a treaty is void if it conflicts with a peremptory norm of general international law from which no derogation is permitted', and one of the examples referred to by the Commission was a treaty contemplating an unlawful use of force contrary to the principles of the Charter. International Law Comm'n, Report U.N. Doc. No. A/5509, at 11-12 (1963). Mr. Kyprianou placed substantial stress on this language in Security Council debates. See 19 U.N. SCOR, 1098th meeting 18 (1964). But it is relevant only to the extent that the Charter prohibits armed intervention under Article IV of the Treaty of Guarantee, and, therefore, it adds nothing on that basic question.

Mr. Kyprianou also cited in support of his position a famous passage from the *Corfu Channel Case*, [1949] I.C.J. 4, 35: 'The Court can only regard the alleged right of intervention as the manifestation of a policy of force, such as has, in the past, given rise to most serious abuses and such as cannot, whatever be the present defects in international organization, find a place in international law.' See 19 U.N. SCOR, 1098th meeting 18-19 (1964). But the language quoted is inapplicable in the present situation since 'the alleged right of intervention' was based on the United Kingdom's view of its need to secure evidence to present to the Court, rather than on the enforcement of obligations under a

Turkey maintained, however, that military intervention under Article IV of the treaty would not be 'against the territorial integrity and political independence' of Cyprus, since the Treaty of Guarantee was designed to 'insure the maintenance of [Cypriot] independence, territorial integrity and security', and action under the treaty must, in the terms of Article IV, be for 'the sole aim of re-establishing the state of affairs created by the . . . Treaty'.[36] This argument had substantial appeal on the issue whether the *first* qualifying phrase in Article 2(4) prohibits *all* uses of force under Article IV. The question remained, however, whether military intervention under Article IV could ever be consistent with the 'Purposes of the United Nations', and, if so, under what circumstances and in what manner. Turkey did not meet this issue squarely.

The Charter lists the maintenance of 'international peace and security' first among the organization's Purposes. 'Primary responsibility' for effecting this Purpose is assigned to the Security Council by Article 2(4). Both the General Assembly and regional arrangements are also given express authority to maintain the peace in certain situations, but the Article 51 reference to the 'inherent right' of self-defence is the only explicit Charter acknowledgement that nations may separately employ force. On this basis some commentators have concluded that all unilateral uses of force, except in self-defence, are absolutely prohibited.[37] That is a persuasive approach to many states. Apart from questions concerning the scope and content of the self-defence exception, it establishes a broad and certain mandate for the peaceful resolution of international conflict, clearly a fundamental interest of the organization as a whole. Moreover, this view seems consistent with the negotiating history of the Charter.[38]

---

treaty that specifically authorizes, in the Turkish view, armed intervention for that purpose.

Note that although Article 2(1) was inapplicable to Cyprus until it became a member of the United Nations in 1960, see U.N. General Assembly Res. No. 1489, 15 U.N. GAOR, Supp. 16, at 65 (A/4684) (1960), Article 2(4) limits the actions of members against 'any state', whether or not a member.

[36] 20 U.N. SCOR, 1234th meeting 23–4 (1965).

[37] See the authorities cited and the critique of their views in Stone, *Aggression and World Order* 92–103 (1958).

[38] '[T]he unilateral use of force or similar coercive measures is not authorized or admitted. The use of arms in legitimate self-defense remains admitted and unimpaired. The use of force, therefore, remains legitimate only to back up

Turkey had never answered this line of analysis in any of the previous Security Council debates. Its representatives knew that an answer would be needed if they were to justify an attack under Article IV. Further, the support of the United Kingdom would also be essential. The argument would be difficult enough in all events; without the endorsement of another Guarantor Power it would be virtually impossible to sustain.

B. PRESSURES FROM THE UNITED KINGDOM

As in the past, Britain's primary interest in the crisis that began in late 1963 was to keep the peace. Its strategic role around the world was slowly waning, but Cyprus and the two British bases on the Island were still important. The bases continued to serve as part of the NATO 'shield' and as protection for England's Middle Eastern oil supplies as well. The renewal of violence on the Island, and particularly the possibility of a direct military clash between Greece and Turkey, endangered those interests. Further, England had special responsibilities as a Guarantor Power. The scope and dimensions of those responsibilities were unclear, but they at least called on Britain to exert every possible pressure to keep peace on the Island.

The British representative's response to Mr. Kyprianou's question carried the clear implication that, in certain circumstances, the treaty did authorize the use of force and that such use would not necessarily be inconsistent with the United Nations Charter. But he added that 'it is . . . not part of our present task in this Council to consider hypothetical situations . . . The urgent task of this Council is . . . [to find] the best way of ensuring that occasion for interventions under Article IV would never arise.'[39]

Great Britain had never publicly declared the circumstances in which intervention would be appropriate. But, as we have seen, British officials had claimed that the Guarantor Powers could act as a 'regional arrangement' under Chapter VIII of the Charter. Support for this general position, and in opposition to the Cypriot arguments, could be drawn along the following lines.

---

the decisions of the Organization at the start of a controversy or during its solution in the way that the Organization itself ordains.' Doc. No. 944, I/1/34(1), 6 U.N. Conf. Int'l Org. Docs. 446, 459 (1945) (report of Rapporteur of Committee 1 to Commission I).

[39] 19 U.N. SCOR, 1098th meeting 12 (1964).

Although the negotiating history of the United Nations Charter indicates that its drafters intended to preclude the unilateral use of force except in self-defence, that history must be viewed in terms of the peacekeeping scheme projected by the Charter's framers. Under that scheme, the five permanent Council members would co-operate in policing the world. It is doubtful whether the Council could have fulfilled this vision even if the American–Soviet solidarity postulated at San Francisco had lasted. In all events, the United Nations members had the wisdom and ingenuity to develop other machinery for giving effect to the organization's purposes. They viewed the Charter as a constitutive document of considered generality designed to deal with new and changing circumstances. The decline of the Security Council was matched by the growth of the peacekeeping capabilities of the General Assembly, through the 'Uniting for Peace Resolution', and of regional arrangements under Chapter VIII. United Nations members were conscious of the issues concerning those arrangements and the limitations on their actions, for United States representatives had recently contended that the Rio Treaty of 1947 provided a sound legal basis for the 1962 quarantine of Cuba under Chapter VIII.[40] Analysis of the terms of the Treaty of Guarantee and the intent of its drafters suggests that the treaty, and perhaps similar agreements,[41] provides a

---

[40] See Chayes, 'Law and the Quarantine of Cuba', 41 Foreign Affairs 550, 554–7 (1963); Meeker, 'Defensive Quarantine and the Law', 57 Am. J. Int'l L. 515, 518–19.

[41] Only a few treaties of guarantee, in the traditional sense, appear to have been concluded in this century, although they were once a relatively frequent form of international undertaking. See the agreements cited in McNair, *The Law of Treaties* 239–54 (1961); 1 Oppenheim, *International Law* 964–8 (8th ed., Lauterpacht, 1955). None of these examples seems sufficiently analogous in both their terms and the circumstances in which they were concluded to warrant analysis here. Two points concerning this class of treaties should, however, be mentioned. First, several agreements, such as the Treaty of Locarno, 16 Oct. 1925, 54 L.N.T.S. 289 (signed by Germany, Belgium, Great Britain, France, and Italy), included both individual and collective guarantees. See Bishop, 'The Locarno Pact', 11 Transact. Grot. Soc'y 79, 95–6 (1926). Second, particular constitutions were among the subjects of protection of several early treaties of guarantee. In connection with such agreements, Sir Robert Phillimore wrote that 'a Right of Intervention has been, and may be conceded by one nation to another, without entailing the loss of legal personality in the nation which concedes it—without reducing that nation to the *status* . . . of a State so protected as to be dependent.

'This is a construction of Guaranteeship opposed certainly to every presump-

mechanism analogous to regional arrangements for the use of force consistent with the Purposes of the United Nations.

The basic aim of the 1960 Accords was to protect the Turkish Cypriot minority and to establish conditions for the preservation of peace on an island riven by violence for centuries. The Accords provided a carefully conceived structure of guarantees designed to achieve that purpose. The internal guarantees included in the Constitution were the first line of defence against intercommunal strife. But if these guarantees were not enforced, the mechanism of protection established in the Treaty of Guarantee was to come into operation—collective measures or, if multilateral agreement were not possible, unilateral action.

The arrangements contemplated under Chapter VIII concern affairs within a region rather than a single nation. This is a somewhat arid distinction, however, since violation of the Treaty of Guarantee could lead to a conflict involving three Mediterranean nations as well as the United Kingdom with its significant interests in the Mediterranean area. More important, specific recognition of a right of unilateral action distinguishes the Treaty of Guarantee from the constitutive documents of regional arrangements.[42] Agreements such as the Rio Treaty require at least the assent of a majority of their members for action under the aegis of the collectivity. The basic rationale for the use of force under regional arrangements is that 'decisions are made by political processes involving checks and balances and giving assurance that the outcome will reflect considered judgment and broad consensus'.[43] The unilateral decisions of the Guarantor Power under Article IV provide no such assurance. On the contrary, individual action may not occur under the terms of Article IV unless the Guarantor Powers are unable to agree on joint measures.

At the same time, however, the treaty requirement of consulta-

---

tion of public law, and one which can only be created—if, according to modern practice and usage, it can be created at all—by express words. Such a Treaty is fraught with mischief to the best interests both of Public and International Law.' 2 Phillimore, *International Law* 85 (1882). (Emphasis in original.)

[42] Another distinguishing feature is that the operative provisions of Article IV are not triggered unless one of the *parties* violates the terms of the treaty. Other regional arrangements, such as the Inter-American System, to the extent they permit the use of force, are concerned primarily with meeting threats of non-member intervention within the region.

[43] Chayes, 'Law and the Quarantine of Cuba', 41 Foreign Affairs 550, 554 (1963).

tion does ensure a cooling-off period and an opportunity to weigh the views of all Guarantor Powers before unilateral action is taken. Furthermore, Article IV includes an important limitation on the action that may be taken pursuant to it. Such action must be 'with the sole aim of re-establishing the state of affairs created by the present Treaty'. Implicit in the restriction is a requirement that the measures taken be appropriate to that 'sole aim'.

On this basis, Great Britain could reasonably conclude, in certain circumstances, that the consensual arrangement embodied in the Treaty of Guarantee authorizes the use of force to re-establish the 'state of affairs'. It also might reasonably judge that such forcible action was consistent with the Purposes of the United Nations and with Article 2(4) of the Charter. Whether the legal basis would be found in Chapter VIII or in analogy to that Chapter was less important to Turkey than the possibility of British support.

Assuming that the United Kingdom would continue to maintain the view that unilateral intervention by a Guarantor Power was appropriate in certain circumstances, could Turkey reasonably predict that British officials would find the situation, in early August 1964, within those circumstances? At that time the Security Council had been seized of the crisis for more than six months. Under resolutions of 4 March, 13 March, and 20 June 1964, it was actively exercising jurisdiction over the matter.[44] By the first of these resolutions a United Nations peacekeeping force was on the Island, a mediator had been appointed by the Secretary-General, and all United Nations members had been called upon to 'refrain from any action or threat of action likely to worsen the situation in the sovereign Republic of Cyprus, or to endanger international peace'.

[44] See U.N. Docs. No. S/5575, S/5603, S/5778 (1964).
At the time the Irish Government agreed to provide troops for the United Nations Peacekeeping Force in Cyprus, the Minister of External Affairs of Ireland wrote to the Secretary-General: 'The Government have asked me to make it clear that it is our expectation that if during the presence of the United Nations force in Cyprus the Governments of Great Britain, Greece and Turkey, or any one of them, should intervene, or attempt to impose by force or by threat of force a solution of the problem, and particularly a solution by partition, immediate steps will be taken to withdraw the Irish contingent from Cyprus.' Quoted in Press Release of the Permanent Mission of Ireland to the United Nations, 24 Mar. 1964. The Turkish Government must have realized, therefore, that unilateral military intervention might trigger the collapse of the peacekeeping force.

The United Kingdom had urged Security Council consideration of the crisis and had sponsored creation of the peacekeeping
force. England had supported each step by the Secretary-General;
in fact, it had counselled him to take stronger measures. In this
light, it must have seemed likely that Great Britain would consider Council involvement in the crisis to have pre-empted
Guarantor Power authority to decide to use force under the
Treaty of Guarantee. Having called on the Council to fulfil its
peacekeeping obligations under the Charter, Britain presumably
would conclude that the right to act unilaterally was in abeyance.
Article 53 of the United Nations Charter provides that 'no enforcement action shall be taken under regional arrangements or
by regional agencies without the authorization of the Security
Council . . .' The steps taken by the Security Council seem to bar
any argument that this condition had been satisfied. Quite apart
from whether armed intervention by a regional arrangement
requires prior and express Security Council authorization—
questions raised in the Cuban missile crisis—Article 53 appears
to preclude military action by a regional arrangement once the
Council has authorized creation of a peacekeeping force to deal
with a crisis.[45] In this sense, the Treaty of Guarantee and the
Charter form a hierarchical structure in which the narrower institution's processes may be pre-empted by those of the broader. If
the treaty is viewed as creating a mechanism analogous to a
regional arrangement rather than an institution precisely within
the terms of Chapter VIII, the pre-emption analysis is, if anything, more persuasive.

Turkey could have responded that some standard of effective
exercise of Council jurisdiction should be applied, and that the
existence of the United Nations Force in Cyprus should not pre-

[45] At the outset of the Cuban missile crisis, the United States Department of
State claimed that the quarantine was not 'enforcement action' because such
action involves an obligation to use force and the O.A.S. (Organization of
American States) Organ of Consultation could (and did) do no more than
recommend the use of force under the Rio Treaty; the Expenses Case was cited
as authority. See Department of State Memorandum, Legal Basis for the Quarantine of Cuba, 23 Oct. 1962, reprinted in Chayes, Ehrlich, and Lowenfeld,
International Legal Process, Documents Supplement 552–8 (1968). But in later analyses,
the State Department Legal Adviser implicitly shifted position, acknowledging
that the quarantine could be viewed as 'enforcement action', but arguing that
the necessary Security Council authorization need be neither prior nor express
and that it had been obtained. See Chayes, 'Law and the Quarantine of
Cuba', 41 *Foreign Affairs* 550, 555–7 (1963).

clude armed intervention by a Guarantor Power if the force is
unable to deal with the crisis. In this situation, the Cypriot
Government had denied the force the right to exercise its mandate. In fact, the Government's attack against Turkish Cypriots
in the Kokkina–Mansoura area violated an express agreement
with the force commander.

  None the less, it probably seemed unlikely to Turkish officials
that such an argument would be persuasive to Great Britain.
Assuming that in certain circumstances the Turkish use of force
would be compatible with its Charter obligations, England
would probably insist that the burden of proving those circumstances was a heavy one. In terms of the Council's resolution of
4 March, would military intervention 'worsen the situation' from
the standpoint of the international community? In terms of the
Treaty of Guarantee, could the intervention be fairly described
as 'an action with the sole aim of re-establishing the state of
affairs created by the present Treaty'? Apart from the resolution
and the treaty, would the military action be reasonably related
to its purported purpose—to prevent further repressive measures
against Turkish Cypriots? Answers to these and similar questions
could vary depending on the kind of force employed, how it was
used, and other aspects of the precise circumstances. But particularly without an extended opportunity to present the facts, the
chances of persuading Britain must have seemed slim. To admit
the Turkish case would be to acknowledge that the United
Nations was unable to handle the problem effectively. All of
England's actions from the time it brought the crisis to the Council indicated that it would not accept this judgement.

C. PRESSURES FROM THE UNITED STATES

  Like England, the United States had a strong interest in the
peaceful resolution of the crisis. As the most powerful member of
NATO, the United States had substantial responsibilities to
keep the peace among its allies. Those responsibilities were
focused by repeated Soviet charges that the crisis would never
have begun had the NATO bloc not involved itself in the
domestic affairs of the sovereign Republic of Cyprus.

  Beyond those concerns, the United States was inexorably involved in the affair because, since the Truman Plan, it had supplied both Turkey and Greece with virtually all their military

equipment and had trained their armed forces.[46] Between 1948
and 1964, more than 2.3 billion dollars of United States military
assistance was provided to Turkey and approximately 1.3 billion
dollars to Greece.[47]

Resistance to Communism was the primary motivation of
United States military aid under the Truman Plan. The United
States did not intend that its assistance be used against Cyprus or
in defence of Cyprus against Turkey.[48] Twice before August 1964
the United States had dissuaded Turkey from invading the
Island only by the strongest diplomatic pressures. On the second
occasion, in June 1964, President Johnson sent the prime minister,
Mr. Inonu, a secret letter that, in the latter's words, included 'all
the juridical thunderbolts that could be assembled'. The letter
was drafted in the language of legal obligation. The President
claimed that a Turkish invasion of Cyprus would violate a number of international commitments: First, a commitment, of
'complete consultation with the United States before any such
action is taken'; second, a commitment to consult with other
Guarantor Powers, which has 'by no means been exhausted';
third, a commitment to NATO not to undermine the strength of
that organization or to run the risk of involving the Soviet Union;
and fourth, a commitment to the United Nations to act in a
manner consistent with its efforts to bring peace to the Island.
The President's 'juridical thunderbolts' also included the claim
that:

Under Article IV of the agreement with Turkey of July 1947, your
government is required to obtain United States' consent for the use of
military assistance for purposes other than those for which assistance
was furnished . . . I must tell you in all candor that the United States
cannot agree to the use of any United States supplied military equipment
for a Turkish intervention in Cyprus under present circumstances.

In fact, the 1947 United States–Turkey Aid Agreement gives
only the most general rationale for the assistance programme:

[46] See Hearings on the Foreign Assistance Act of 1964 Before the House
Committee on Foreign Affairs, 88th Cong., 2nd Sess. pt. IV, at 501–2 (1964);
Hearings on the Foreign Assistance Act of 1963 Before the Senate Committee
on Foreign Relations, 88th Cong., 1st Sess. 638 (1963).

[47] See Agency for International Development and Department of Defense,
Proposed Mutual Defense and Development Programs FY 1966, Summary
Presentation to the Congress, Mar. 1965, at 226.

[48] See 19 U.N. SCOR, 1153d meeting 7–9 (1964) (statement by Ambassador
Stevenson).

'to achieve the basic purposes of the Charter of the United Nations . . . and strengthen the ties of friendship between the American and Turkish peoples'.[49] On the face of it there is nothing to indicate that military assistance furnished under the Agreement must be used against Communist aggression only, that it must be employed solely for defensive purposes, or even that it cannot be used against an ally of the United States.

At the same time, the Agreement does provide that the assistance 'to be provided' will be withdrawn if the President determines that withdrawal would be 'in the interest of the United States'.[50] It is unclear from the wording of the Agreement whether the United States' right of 'withdrawal' includes withdrawal of assistance already provided to Turkey or whether the right operates prospectively only. As a practical matter, it is hard to imagine how the United States would withdraw assistance previously provided. But Turkish leaders presumably considered the risk of a prospective termination in analysing the advantages and disadvantages of military intervention. A refusal to furnish repair and replacement parts might have been almost as effective within a short period as the removal of equipment already provided. A suspension of United States assistance to Turkey would have seriously jeopardized that country's military strength. The United States' legal authority to take the step was clear. In weighing the matter, Turkey had to consider the opposing pressures on the United States. Failure to terminate assistance could undercut whatever credibility the threat would have in the future.

---

[49] Aid Agreement With Turkey, 12 July 1947, T.I.A.S. No. 1629. This Agreement is similar to the United States Aid Agreement With Greece, but substantially different from the economic co-operation agreements concluded with Turkey, Greece, and other countries in 1948 and thereafter. See, e.g., Economic Cooperation Agreement With Turkey, 4 July 1948, T.I.A.S. No. 1794, as amended, 31 Jan. 1950, T.I.A.S. No. 2037, 16 Aug. 1951, T.I.A.S. No. 2392, 30 Dec. 1952, T.I.A.S. No. 2742.

[50] Id., Art. IV(3). Article III of the Agreement of Co-operation With Turkey, 5 Mar. 1959, T.I.A.S. No. 4191, provides that 'the Government of Turkey undertakes to utilize such military and economic assistance as may be provided by the Government of the United States . . . for the purpose of effectively promoting the economic development of Turkey and preserving its national independence and integrity'. And paragraph 2 of the Mutual Security Agreement With Turkey, 7 Jan. 1952, T.I.A.S. No. 2621, sets forth six general undertakings by the Turkish Government, including 'appropriate steps to insure the effective utilization of the economic and military assistance provided by the United States'.

On the other hand, stopping aid might lose what leverage the United States still had over Turkey's actions.

The United States could have been expected to press all the arguments in President Johnson's June letter. But the United States influence over Turkish affairs had been substantially depleted as a result of the crisis. President Johnson and Mr. Inonu had met in the wake of the aborted invasion in June. Their joint communiqué had stated that their discussions had proceeded on the basis of 'the binding effects of existing treaties'.[51] But having twice dissuaded Turkey from carrying out her military plans, the United States assumed, at least in Turkish eyes, an obligation to resolve the conflict in some other way and on terms favourable to Turkey. Any pressure that induces a nation to forgo the catharsis of self-help generates demands for peaceful change. And in the end, whether the pressure is the persuasive power of another country or the injunction of the Security Council, it can be effective only if it develops modes for peaceful change. But the United States had failed to meet these demands in the Cyprus crisis, though not for want of trying. As a result, numerous anti-American demonstrations had been staged in Ankara throughout the summer of 1964,[52] and there was strong opposition in the Turkish press to United States efforts to restrain Turkey from military intervention. Further, Turkey and the Soviet Union appeared to be developing closer relations. The country that was at one time America's staunchest Near-Eastern ally was reconsidering her interests. To a degree at least, this may be an example of what seems an increasingly common phenomenon—perhaps not a bad one: a maturing nation, closely allied to the United States and substantially dependent on American assistance, realizing that the United States cannot have an unlimited commitment to it—no matter how closely it has adhered to American policy interests.

D. THE TURKISH DECISION

Turkish bombers attacked the Island on 7 and 8 August 1964. The Turkish Government claimed that the bombings were directed solely against military targets,[53] but reports from United Nations representatives in the field concluded that '[t]hese raids

[51] Dep't of State Bull. 49 (1964).
[52] See N.Y. Times, 29 Aug. 1964, p. 1, col. 7.
[53] See 19 U.N. SCOR, 1142d meeting 12 (1964).

on defenseless people killed and maimed many innocent civilians, destroyed much property . . .'[54] On 9 August the Security Council denounced the Turkish action and issued an appeal 'to the Government of Turkey to cease instantly the bombardment and the use of military force of any kind against Cyprus . . .'[55] All its members apparently considered the bombings inconsistent with the Council's cognizance of the crisis, its specific mandate to the parties to refrain from action likely to endanger international peace, and the Charter purpose of maintaining that peace.

Until 7 August 1964, Turkey had complied with the Council's appeal. Until then, Turkey had not used force, although it had threatened to do so on several occasions. In part, Turkey was deterred from carrying out its threats because they had been sufficient to deter the Cypriot Government from cutting off Turkish Cypriot strongholds. In part, Turkey had not acted because of the strong pressures of the Security Council and its members, particularly the United States. Most important, the existence of the United Nations peacekeeping force on the Island had helped to check unilateral action by Turkey. But Turkish representatives had insisted that the United Nations peacekeeping force must not only be operational but also effective in implementing its mandate. When those conditions were no longer met, Turkey concluded that it must act.

In retrospect, some military action by Turkey seems to have been almost inevitable if the continued threat of force was to remain plausible. The United Nations debates before August 1964 reflect, on the part of nations not directly involved, a growing weariness with the crisis and an increasing sense that the people of Cyprus should be left alone to work things out. Turkey's leaders may have concluded that it could no longer cry wolf and be believed.

The preceding analysis has suggested that at the time Turkey probably saw little likelihood of sustaining an appeal in the Security Council for support of any military action based on the Treaty of Guarantee. Turkish representatives knew, therefore, that they would have to turn to a claim of self-defence. To state

[54] Secretary-General, Report on the United Nations' Operation in Cyprus, U.N. Doc. No. 5950, at 64 (1964).

[55] Security Council Res. 193, U.N. Doc. No. S/5868 (1964). See also the consensus adopted by the Council on 11 Aug. 1964. 19 U.N. SCOR, 1143d meeting 62 (1964).

that claim without reference to Article 51 would avoid the need to meet arguments that the measures taken by the Security Council precluded action under the Charter provision and that there had been no 'armed attack against a Member of the United Nations'. In deciding what force to use and how to use it, the Turkish Government presumably sought to act in ways most consistent with a legal case based on the inherent right of self-defence. They sought a limited armed intervention that would have the maximum chance of forcing the Cypriot Government to check its own military efforts, that would underscore the credibility of future threats, and that could be terminated when those objectives were achieved.

The Turkish Government probably considered an invasion of Cyprus as the major alternative to a bombing attack; Turkey had threatened to invade several times before. In weighing the two, an air attack had some obvious military advantages. A landing force would be met by the Cypriot National Guard, by the Greek contingent stationed on Cyprus under the Treaty of Alliance, and by additional Greek troops on the Island in violation of the Treaty of Alliance. Cyprus had no planes and Turkey's air force was three times as strong as that of Greece. The distance between Cyprus and Greece meant that Greek fighter planes could remain over the Island for only a very limited time. Further, it is difficult to call off an invasion without the appearance of a retreat; bombing raids can be terminated much more easily. Apart from those advantages, Turkey could claim that bombings were intended solely to defend the besieged Turkish Cypriots and that they would stop when their safety was assured. In the Turkish representative's statements to the Security Council after the bombings, he stressed the mistreatment of Turkish Cypriots by the Makarios Government and the inability of either the United Nations or the Guarantor Powers acting collectively to protect the Turkish Cypriots.

The Turks of Cyprus, robbed of all their constitutional guarantees, turned upon and massacred by a fratricidal, tyrannical and illegitimate clique of their compatriots, with the other guaranteeing Powers unwilling or unable to act, and with the United Nations Force rendered impotent, had nowhere to turn for protection but to Turkey, and Turkey could not ignore such a humane and legitimate call.

... In these circumstances the Turkish Government has been compelled to stop the flow of reinforcements by bombing from the air the road used for the purpose of bringing them in. This action undertaken by Turkish aircraft is directed exclusively at military targets and constitutes a limited police action taken in legitimate self-defense.[56]

This was the only occasion during the entire crisis that began in December 1963, that a Turkish representative publicly referred to self-defence as a basis for military action.

Turkey must have expected strong pressures to halt the bombings. The likelihood of overwhelming condemnation by the Security Council was probably a dominant consideration. Against those pressures, Turkey could expect—at the very least—that its future threats would be credible. Further, it could condition agreement to halt the bombings on the Cypriot Government's agreement to end its siege of the Kokkina-Mansoura area. According to the Turkish representative to the United Nations, that is precisely what happened:

At the time when Turkey agreed to discontinue air intervention at the Kokkina–Mansoura area, Turkey had been given to understand that the Greek Cypriot aggressors would withdraw to the positions they occupied prior to August 5, that the safety of the Turkish Cypriots in that area would be secured and that the inhuman economic blockade applied against the Turks of Cyprus would be lifted.[57]

[56] 19 U.N. SCOR, 1142d meeting 11–12 (1964).
[57] U.N. Doc. No. S/5954, at 1 (1964). In this document, a memorandum to the Secretary-General, the Turkish Government declared that the quoted conditions were not met and that, therefore, Turkey would deliver food to those subject to the blockade. Furthermore, it threatened that if the deliveries were prevented, 'the Turkish Government will be compelled to take appropriate action in order to defend its rights and carry out the humanitarian duties which devolve upon it'. The Secretary-General immediately responded that the Security Council's resolution of 9 Aug. and the Council consensus of 11 Aug. contained no reference to an understanding such as that referred to in the Turkish memorandum and that '[i]mplementation of the resolutions of the Security Council and of the Council consensus of 11 August cannot be made contingent on compliance by the parties with any provisions extraneous to these texts'. U.N. Doc. No. S/5961, at 2 (1964). He emphasized that UNFICYP was doing all that it could to help in bringing food to the Turkish Cypriots in the Kokkina area, but that 'in order to make possible such UNFICYP assistance, any plans by the Turkish Government for bringing supplies into Cypriot territory must have the consent of the Cyprus Government'. Id. at 3–4. And he drew 'attention to the possible dangerous consequences of any attempt to bring materials or supplies into Cypriot territory on any other basis'. Id. at 4. The Turkish Government never carried out its threat.

In sum, Turkey claimed that since the United Nations peace-keeping force could not protect the Turkish Cypriots, bombing was Turkey's only recourse. In fact, Turkey bombed and the fighting in the Kokkina–Mansoura area stopped.

V

THE
GREEK GOVERNMENT'S DECISION
IN 1967 TO WITHDRAW ITS TROOPS
FROM CYPRUS

THE 1960 Treaty of Alliance stipulates that not more than 950 Greek troops shall be stationed on Cyprus. In the wake of the crisis that began on Christmas Day 1963, however, large numbers of Greek forces as well as arms were brought to the Island. By 1967, upwards of ten to twelve thousand Greek soldiers—estimates vary—were stationed on Cyrpus.[1] They were led by General George Grivas, who still openly called for enosis. General Grivas had returned to Cyprus from Greece in 1964 as Supreme Commander of the Cypriot Defence Forces. Those Forces also included the Cypriot National Guard, which had some 10,000 active soldiers and 20,000 reserves. The enlisted men were mainly Greek Cypriots, but many commissioned and non-commissioned officers were mainland Greeks.

On 15 November 1967, the National Guard launched an attack against several Turkish Cypriot positions. The attacks brought not only strong protests from the United Nations Secretary-General and force commander, but also a new threat of invasion by Turkey. A ceasefire was negotiated within 24 hours, but the new crisis was not resolved until 10 days of intense international negotiations produced an agreement by the Greek Government to withdraw all its troops on Cyprus in excess of the 950-man contingent authorized by the Treaty of Alliance. This Chapter examines the Greek Government's decision and the impact of legal norms and institutions on the process of decision-making. The analysis suggests that law provided both a framework for Turkey's insistence that Greece reaffirm the 1960 Accords by withdrawing its excess forces and also a mechanism for Greece

[1] Some reports indicated that 20,000 Greek troops had come to Cyprus, see *N.Y. Times*, 19 Nov. 1967, p. 14, col. 6, but most estimates were in the 10,000 to 12,000 range.

to accede to Turkey without being humiliated and without armed conflict.

Tension had risen and eased on the Island in the three years after the Turkish bombings in August 1964. Periodically, the Cypriot Government would make a new effort to choke off the Turkish Cypriot enclaves, Turkey would renew its threat to land troops, the United Nations Security Council and Secretary-General would make an urgent appeal for restraint on all sides, the Cypriot Government would relax its pressures, and Turkish armed forces would be demobilized. The United Nations force remained on the Island, though reduced in strength to some 4,500 men. Isolated shooting incidents occurred daily, but the United Nations troops were, with a few exceptions, able to check large-scale outbreaks of violence. Further, United Nations representatives sought to mediate between the two communities in an effort to restore at least a semblance of normality to Cypriot economic and political life.

In the summer of 1965, for example, the Greek Cypriot members of the Council of Ministers, under the chairmanship of President Makarios, proposed legislation to abolish all communal distinctions regarding elections for the Presidency, Vice-Presidency, and membership in the House.[2] The legislation was adopted by the House after the Turkish Cypriot Representatives had been refused the right to participate in the House proceeding. Diplomatic protests were made by both the British and Turkish Governments. At a subsequent Security Council meeting the French, Soviet, and United States representatives as well as those of England and Turkey, were all critical of the Cypriot action.[3] Even the Greek representatives suggested that 'one might conceivably have some misgivings as to the timing' of the legislation.[4] In these circumstances, the Cypriot Government backed away from the scheme.

A few months later, the pendulum swung the other way. The Cypriot Government took several steps that seemed to mark a shift from its prior intransigence *vis-à-vis* both the Turkish Cypriots and Turkey. Perhaps most important, it declared in October 1965 'that it is ready and willing' to: (a) adopt a Code

[2] See Secretary-General, Report on Recent Developments in Cyprus. U.N. Doc. No. S/6569 (1965).

[3] 20 U.N. SCOR, 1235th meeting (1965).

[4] 20 U.N. SCOR, 1234th meeting 17 (1965).

of Fundamental Rights, along the lines of the Universal Declaration of Human Rights, to protect the Turkish Cypriots; (b) allow the Turkish Cypriot community sole control over the 'education, culture, religion, [and] personal status' of its members; (c) permit Turkish Cypriots 'participation in Parliament' on the basis of proportionate representation; and (d) accept, for a transitional period, a United Nations Commissioner on the Island and other 'appropriate machinery' to ensure enforcement of the rights of Turkish Cypriots.[5] The extent of practical protection that would be afforded Turkish Cypriots under the Code of Fundamental Rights may be open to some question, particularly in light of the difficulties faced in enforcing the far more detailed statement of Fundamental Rights and Liberties in the 1960 Constitution. The step may be explained in part by the Cypriot Government's desire in the months preceding the opening of the General Assembly's twentieth session to gain support for its position on the various issues in the crisis. At the same time, the declaration as a whole seemed to represent a significant effort by the Government to meet some of the legitimate concerns of the Turkish Cypriots.

Similarly, the Turkish Cypriot community, supported by Turkey, seemed to fluctuate between efforts at separatism and reconciliation. The Cypriot Government continued to charge that Turkey was forcing Turkish Cypriots into enclaves—preventing them from returning to their homes—to maintain bargaining strength for partition as the ultimate solution. Turkey continued to claim that the Cypriot Government, supported by Greece, was still pressing toward enosis.

The United Nations presence on Cyprus served to check recourse to armed force, but it only palliated some symptoms of the crisis and reached none of its basic causes. The Peacekeeping Force had been an important moderating element, and had used its good offices in numerous ways, such as bringing food to Turkish Cypriot refugees. But it had not been able to take effective measures even to reduce the means by which fighting could occur in the future. It had no authority to disarm, to arrest, or to prohibit the importation of military equipment; it was, therefore, powerless to act in some areas where action was needed. Yet it was clear that Archbishop Makarios opposed any expansion of the force's mandate to give it the necessary authority, and that the Soviet

[5] See U.N. Doc. No. A/6039 (1965).

Union would veto such a proposal unless it had the Archbishop's approval. The Security Council periodically renewed the limited mandate of the force and urged the parties involved to find a speedy solution. But the very reliance that each side placed on the United Nations may have reduced their sense of urgency to find a long-run solution.

At the same time, the crisis had serious consequences outside the Island. Among the most troublesome was the impact on Greek Orthodox inhabitants of Turkey. Most of them live in Istanbul and most are Turkish citizens. Like the Moslem minority in Greece, they are protected by provisions in the Treaty of Lausanne.[6] By an agreement of 1930, Greek nationals in Turkey and Turkish nationals in Greece were also granted the right to practise vocations otherwise reserved for each country's citizens.[7] In March 1964 the Turkish Government announced that it would abrogate the 1930 agreement and expelled a number of Greek nationals from Istanbul. It acknowledged that retaliation for Greek support of the Cypriot Government was the prime motivation.[8]

Throughout 1965 and 1966 the Cyprus affair was in constant flux. Neither Archbishop Makarios nor the Turkish leaders were prepared to go very far to stabilize the situation. An event in Greece in the spring of 1967, however, may have had a more profound impact on the long-term outcome of the crisis than any of the Cypriot or Turkish machinations.

On 21 April 1967, a military junta took over the Greek Government in a bloodless *coup*. The junta declared a state of emergency and suspended key provisions of the Constitution. The takeover was the culmination of a prolonged political crisis between King Constantine and the royalist parties on the one hand and the Centre Union Party of George Papandreou on the other. The Centre Union Government had fallen in July 1965 over charges that Andreas Papandreou, son of the premier, was involved in a plot by leftist army officers to seize power. New elections were

[6] Treaty of Lausanne, 24 July 1923, Part I, sec. III, 28 L.N.T.S. 11 (1924).

[7] Convention of Establishment, Commerce and Navigation Between Greece and Turkey, 30 Oct. 1930, Art. 4, 125 L.N.T.S. 371 (1931).

[8] 19 U.N. SCOR, 1146th meeting 18 (1946). Turkey also sought to prove discrimination against Moslems in Greece. Compare *Turkish Minority in Greece, Greek Minority in Turkey* (undated pamphlet distributed by the Turkish Embassy in Washington), with Greek Information Services, *The Greek Minority in Turkey and the Turkish Minority in Greece*, Jan. 1965.

scheduled for the end of May 1967, and it appeared that George Papandreou would probably gain enough popular support to force the king to ask him to form a new cabinet. The *coup*, of course, eliminated that possibility.

International reaction to the military takeover was immediate and adverse. Protests against a dictatorship in the birthplace of democracy were heard around the world, from democracies and dictatorships alike. The United States imposed a selective embargo on shipments under its military aid programme. Some $80 million in military equipment had been earmarked for Greece under that programme, but key items such as tanks and aeroplanes were withheld. President Johnson reportedly told the new Greek Ambassador to the United States that Greece could not count on a resumption of military aid unless it returned to constitutional democracy.[9]

The other NATO countries were even sharper in their expressions of concern. Denmark, for example, announced that it would raise the Greek issue at the next NATO Council of Ministers meeting. The Danish Government expressed the hope that 'Greece will return in the shortest time to a free and democratic situation'.[10] Reactions in the European Economic Community were no less strong. The EEC Parliament unanimously adopted an unprecedented resolution in which it declared that the Association Agreement with Greece could not be implemented fully as long as the country lacked freely elected governmental institutions.[11] Further, in September 1967 the Governments of Denmark, Norway, and Sweden instituted an action against Greece before the European Commission on Human Rights.[12] The Scandinavian petition alleged a whole series of offences against the Human Rights Convention. Finally, the Soviet Union was quick to condemn the new Greek régime as part of an 'imperialist' plot to make Cyprus a NATO base for aggression against Communist countries, Arab nations, and national liberation movements.[13]

It is too early to measure the full impact of the Greek *coup* on the Cyrprus crisis. But some effects were readily determinable soon

[9] *The Times* (London) 26 Sept. 1967, p. 1, col. 1.
[10] 62 Am. J. Int'l L. 449 (1968).
[11] Id. at 448.   [12] Id. at 441.
[13] See Adams and Cottrell, *Cyprus Between East and West* 51 (1968), quoting from *Pravda*, 5 July 1967.

after the takeover. Perhaps most significant, relations between Archbishop Makarios and the Greek régime were less than warm from the start. If the Archbishop had in fact dreamed of becoming the Greek prime minister after enosis, the chance was lost, at least for the time being.

The Papendreou Government had reportedly promised the Archbishop that no steps toward a permanent settlement with Turkey would be taken without his approval. The new régime apparently gave no such assurances. In fact, the Greek military government seemed to have concluded that enosis would be possible only if some territorial concessions were made to Turkey and that union would be worth the price. There were conflicting reports on the settlement terms acceptable to Greece. It may be that Greek leaders were themselves uncertain. In all events, the Archbishop had made it clear that he would not accept partition of the Island under any name. In July 1964, President Johnson had appointed Dean Acheson to act as mediator; Mr. Acheson had proposed enosis plus a Turkish base-area on the Island and guarantees for the Turkish Cypriots. But Archbishop Makarios had scuttled the plan, and nothing had occurred in the two intervening years to make him change his views.[14] A report in 1965 by the United Nations mediator, Mr. Galo Plaza, confirmed that such a scheme was still unacceptable to Greek Cypriots.[15]

Further, it was increasingly apparent that although a majority of Greek Cypriots still had a powerful sense of their ethnic ties to Greece, enosis was a more attractive dream than would be the reality. Many Greek Cypriots were having serious second thoughts about the merits of integration, for they saw it would raise troublesome problems. Rule by a military dictatorship was one obvious difficulty; different systems of law and the administration of justice, different currencies (Cyprus was tied to the pound sterling), different tax and social security structures, and quite different economies were others. Perhaps most important, the standard of living in Cyprus was substantially higher than in Greece. However, no public figure in either country could publicly admit that the Hellenic vision was fading. On the con-

[14] For Mr. Acheson's own account of his efforts, see Acheson, 'Cyprus: The Anatomy of the Problem', 46 Chicago B. Record 349, 352–3 (1965).

[15] See United Nations Mediator on Cyprus, Report to the Secretary-General, U.N. Doc. No. S/6253 (1965).

trary, leaders in both nations continued to proclaim that enosis was their ultimate goal[16]—in spite of the provisions in the Treaty of Guarantee forbidding all activity tending to promote 'directly or indirectly either union . . . or partition of the Island'.

Tensions between the Greek and Cypriot Governments were heightened by the large numbers of mainland Greek soldiers on the Island. The situation was further exacerbated by the growing animosities between the Archbishop and General Grivas. The General had left the Island in disgust in 1959 after the Zurich and London Conferences had apparently ended his hopes for enosis. As the most capable military leader the Island had known, he was allowed to return in 1964, but his relations with the Archbishop were permanently strained. They became worse as the chances for enosis dimmed. Throughout the summer of 1967 there were periodic rumours that the military in Greece wanted to extend its régime to Cyprus, using the Greek forces on the Island. The Archbishop reportedly was suspicious that the General would try to lead a _coup_ to depose him and to declare enosis.[17] These reports were all denied by the Greek Government, but it made no effort to hide its efforts to reach some accommodation with Turkey. In July it issued an official statement calling for the immediate dismissal of Cypriot leaders who 'on the eve of decisive developments' set 'groundless conditions and subversive prerequisites' making enosis problematical.[18]

In September the Greek and Turkish prime ministers met for for the first time in three years; Cyprus was the main topic of discussion. Apparently, the outlines of alternative settlement arrangement were put forward, but the talks ultimately collapsed. Subsequently, representatives of each side agreed that a package had been proposed involving enosis, cession of a portion of the Island to Turkey, and international guarantees for the Turkish Cypriots—much like Mr. Acheson's scheme. But each side publicly claimed that the other had done the proposing.[19]

In the autumn of 1967, the Cypriot Government adopted a series of measures calculated to reduce tensions on the Island.[20]

---

[16] See Brown, 'Cyprus: A Study in Unresolved Conflict', 23 World Today 396, 402–4 (1967).

[17] Salih, _Cyprus: An Analysis of Cypriot Political Discord_ 131 (1968).

[18] _The Times_ (London), 3 July 1967, p. 5, col. 6.

[19] See 22 U.N. SCPR, 1385th meeting 36–7 (1967).

[20] See U.N. Doc. No. S/8286, at 35–8 (1967).

A number of Government fortifications and road blocks near key Turkish Cypriot enclosures were left unmanned. Particularly important was the release by the Cypriot Government of President Denktash of the Turkish Communal Chamber. (Mr. Denktash had left Cyprus soon after the 1963 troubles began, and remained away under threat of prosecution if he returned; he secretly came back in October 1967, and was arrested almost immediately.) But these concessions were more than offset by the new crisis that began in mid-November. According to one report, the release of Mr. Denktash 'was evidently too much for the pride of the Greek Government and in particular of General Grivas . . . Accordingly, with the approval of Athens, he decided evidently to put the Turkish Cypriots in their place, sent two patrols through an important Turkish enclave, and when a few shots were fired at the patrol the National Guard put on a full-scale and obviously deliberate attack . . .'[21] Whether or not this description of motives is correct, the patrols did trigger a major new crisis on Cyprus. As is true of all violent incidents on the Island, Greek and Turkish stories vary on how the trouble began. But the United Nations Secretary-General's reports are clear in placing the blame.[22] According to those reports, the sequence of events was as follows.

Patrols of the 2,000-man Greek Cypriot Police had regularly covered much of the Island since December 1963. After a series of shooting incidents in July 1967, however, the Police on its own initiative stopped patrolling an area on the highway between Nicosia and Limassol, near the village of Ayios Theodhoros. There was at least a tacit agreement between the Cypriot Police and the United Nations Peacekeeping Force that the patrols would not be resumed until the force agreed that tensions had sufficiently eased. The Police pressed for resumption in September 1967, but the Turkish Cypriots objected, claiming that the patrolling should not begin again until the National Guard, dominated by Greek officers, withdrew from a recently created fortification in Larnaca. The force commander argued, however, that the two situations were not related. He finally proposed that the patrols resume gradually, beginning in November. The Turkish Cypriots continued to resist and while the negotiations were going on, the Cyprus Police announced it would start the

[21] *The Times* (London), 29 Nov. 1967, p. 9, col. 8.
[22] See U.N. Docs. No. S/8248/Add. 1–3 (1967).

patrols without waiting for Turkish Cypriot agreement. The United Nations Force commander and the Secretary-General's Special Representative objected, claiming that the release of the President of the Turkish Communal Chamber had opened the way for a permanent easing of tensions on the Island.

The United Nations commander had agreed that if negotiations concerning the patrols ultimately failed, the force would 'take appropriate measures to restore the *status quo ante*' by escorting the patrols. But on the afternoon of 14 November, General Grivas informed the force that the patrols would begin in 25 minutes. The General said that if the United Nations did not protect the patrols, the National Guard would escort them and 'would be prepared to meet whatever consequences resulted'. In fact, the National Guard had already begun large-scale military manoeuvres in the area. In these circumstances, the Secretary-General reported, there could be 'no question' of United Nations escorts. Three patrols proceeded without incident, but a fourth met a Turkish Cypriot roadblock, shots were fired——apparently by Turkish Cypriots—and the National Guard opened up with heavy machine-guns, artillery, and mortars. At the same time, another National Guard attack was launched against a village 2½ miles away. United Nations posts were destroyed by the shelling; National Guard troops dismantled the United Nations radio at one key position, and disarmed the United Nations soldiers at another. United Nations efforts to arrange a ceasefire were ignored until the villages had been virtually overrun. A ceasefire and withdrawal of National Guardsmen was negotiated on 16 November, after strong United Nations protests to the Cypriot Government. In the interim, however, the Turkish Minister of Foreign Affairs issued the following statement:

The attack launched against the Ayios Theodhoros area has introduced an element of complication such as has not been seen since 1964. Such action, while there was still a possibility of reaching a negotiated solution of the Ayios Theodhoros problem (meaning patrolling by the Cyprus Police), constitutes a flagrant provocation by the Cyprus Government. UNFICYP is requested to stop the fighting immediately and clear the Turkish Cypriot areas of Ayios Theodhoros and Kophinou of both Greek Cypriot and Greek armed forces. If this cannot be done, a crisis which will go beyond the borders of the Island will be unavoidable.[23]

[23] Quoted in U.N. Doc. No. S/8248, at 7 (1967).

The incident triggered intense international negotiations that ultimately led to the withdrawal of all Greek troops in excess of the 950-man contingent. The Governments of Turkey, Cyprus, and the United States were all directly involved in those negotiations. Further, the United Nations, and particularly the Secretary-General, played a critical role in the ultimate Greek decision. The pressures of the three foreign Governments are first examined, primarily in terms of the relevance of legal considerations. The decision itself is then analysed with particular focus on the role of the United Nations.

A. PRESSURES FROM TURKEY

In the period from 1964 to 1967, Turkey and the Turkish Cypriots publicly maintained that the Cypriot Republic should become a federation rather than an independent nation unfettered by the 1960 Agreements, as advocated by the Archbishop, or a part of Greece, as urged by the Greek Government.[24] Under the scheme proposed by the Turkish Cypriots, the Island would be divided into two separate territories, and each community would control all governmental functions within its territory except federal concerns such as foreign affairs and banking. But both Greeks and Greek Cypriots claimed that the scheme was just a cover for the real Turkish aim—partition of the Island.[25]

In all events, Turkish leaders must have felt increasing pressures to take some affirmative steps toward a permanent resolu-

[24] The Turkish Cypriot leadership has stated, for example, that 'the Turkish community feels that nothing short of federation . . . could give them adequate guarantees for the future . . . [T]he Turkish federation proposal would not in any way entail the partitioning of the island but would only serve to pave the way for peaceful coexistence and cooperation between the two communities within the framework of a totally independent and sovereign State.' U.N. Doc. No. S/6279, at 7 (1965). Mr. Galo Plaza interpreted the concept of federation in these circumstances as necessitating the geographical division of the two communities into states 'separated by an artificial line cutting through interdependent parts of homogenous areas including . . . the cities of Nicosia and Famagusta'. U.N. Doc. No. S/6253, at 58 (1965); see *N.Y. Times*, 16 Aug. 1964, §4 (News of the Week in Review), p. 4, col. 1 (map). For two analyses of possible federation schemes, see Karpat, 'Solution in Cyprus: Federation', in Institute for Mediterranean Affairs, *The Cyprus Dilemma* 35–54 (1967); Trombetas, 'The Republic of Cyprus: A Federation? The Utility of Structural Federation', in id. at 7–34.

[25] See, e.g., 22 U.N. SCOR, 1383d meeting 1–2, 4–7 (1967). For a brief statement of the Turkish Cypriot position, see Ambassador Galo Plaza's report, U.N. Doc. No. S/6253, at 26–7 (1965).

tion of the crisis. It was a substantial and continuing drain on their time and energies. Large amounts of economic assistance through the Turkish Government and the Red Crescent were required on a continuing basis to maintain the thousands of refugees in Turkish Cypriot areas. The domestic political situation within Turkey was still volatile, and the Government could not ignore the 120,000 Turkish Cypriots, even if its leaders had wanted to.

In October 1965 the Justice Party had won a majority of seats in the Turkish National Assembly. Coalition government disappeared for the first time since 1961 as the prime minister, Mr. Demirel, formed an all Justice-Party cabinet. But the danger of a new military *coup* was still real; the Justice Party had received most of its popular support from former backers of the deposed (and executed) prime minister, Menderes. Army leaders had maintained their neutrality from political affairs during the first two years of Mr. Demirel's rule, and his position was made more secure by the election of the former Chief of Staff, General Sunay, as President. But many key officers were infuriated by the continuing Cyprus stalemate. They reportedly demanded a military solution: If the politicians could not partition the Island by diplomatic means, an invasion could. At the least, an invasion could land a strong Turkish force on the Island to protect the Turkish Cypriots. The proposal was widely suggested in the press, and appeared to have substantial popular support. President Johnson's letter of June 1964 warning Turkey not to invade was revealed in January 1966 and intensified the problem. As time wore on without any apparent progress there was increasing pressure, from the public in general and the military in particular, to reach some settlement. The whole affair was an enervating distraction from other pressing problems facing the Turkish Government.

For several reasons, the autumn of 1967 was a good time for Turkey to press for a Greek move. First, the Greek military appeared to have established a strong régime that would last for some time and would not have to bend with public opinion, as was often true of previous Greek governments on the Cyprus issue. Further, Greece's ties with its traditional allies were seriously weakened as a result of the *coup*. The United States and other Western nations were looking for signs of responsible Greek statesmanship. A step toward easing the tensions with Turkey might qualify.

Second, the Greek and Cypriot Governments seemed to be drifting further apart, and the likelihood that the Archbishop would undercut any agreement between Turkey and Greece—as had apparently happened to the proposals by Mr. Acheson—would be minimized. Finally, there seemed general agreement among the major powers not directly involved in the crisis that the 1960 Accords were the necessary starting-point for negotiating any new settlement. The members of the Security Council had all concluded that the Accords were in desperate need of revision, but they also called for revision by *all* the parties. That had been the consistent view of the British and the United States Governments. In 1965 and after, it had substantial support from other Council members. Even the Soviet Union seemed tacitly to accept it. In these circumstances, Turkey was in an excellent position to press Greece with international backing. It did not argue that the 1960 Accords 'cannot ever be renegotiated and altered, but that this can only be done in the context of new international arrangements again freely negotiated and agreed to'.

On the other hand, Turkish leaders may well have concluded that time was running out. Although the Security Council as a whole seemed to have at least become more neutral in weighing the Turkish and Greek Cypriot positions, the General Assembly in 1965 adopted a resolution calling on all nations 'to respect the sovereignty, unity, independence and territorial integrity of the Republic of Cyprus and to refrain from any intervention directed against it . . .'[26] Analysis of the terms of the resolution reveals the same problems previously considered concerning the application of the Charter's provisions, particularly Articles 2(1) and 2(4), to the exercise of Turkish rights under the Treaty of Guarantee. But Turkey had argued at length against the resolution and considered its adoption a serious blow. By the same token, Cyprus viewed the General Assembly's action as a major victory.[27]

Of more immediate and serious concern, Turkey was troubled by the slow erosion of Turkish Cypriot status as the stalemate continued. The Turkish Government maintained that the 1960

[26] U.N. Doc. No. A/6166, at 14 (1965); 20 GAOR, 1402d meeting 6 (1965).

[27] See 20 GAOR 10 (1965). The Greek prime minister claimed that passage of the resolution meant that 'the struggles carried on jointly with the Republic of Cyprus have been successfully concluded'. *N.Y. Times*, 20 Dec. 1965, p. 15, col. 5.

Accords were still in effect, but as a practical matter the political situation throughout the Island was far different from that envisaged at Zurich and London. Greek Cypriots were in complete control of all machinery of national government. Whether Turkish Cypriots were excluded—as Turkey claimed—or whether they had absented themselves when the crisis began in December 1963—as the Archbishop contended—the fact remained that they did not participate. The longer the dispute continued, the more it seemed that the 'temporary' governmental arrangements instituted in 1964 might well be permanent. Further, the Cypriot Government still maintained an embargo on shipments to Turks of many goods such as building materials. Through the United Nations, Ankara had some success in pressing for the removal of the restrictions, but these efforts necessarily diverted attention from more basic issues.

All these circumstances led to summit talks between the prime ministers of Greece and Turkey in September 1967.[28] The two nations have issued contradictory reports on what was said during the talks, but both agree that they ended in complete failure. Enosis, together with territorial concessions to Turkey, was evidently a principal focus of discussion, and the breakdown of the meeting seemed to mean that this solution was precluded, at least for a time. As a result, the chance of a bipartite settlement without involving the Archbishop appeared further away than ever. At the same time, pressures within Turkey for some positive step by the Government were steadily increasing.

Whether or not these forces by themselves would have led to a Turkish threat to use force is questionable, but it seems likely that Government leaders believed that some affirmative move by either Greece or Cyprus was essential to meet mounting domestic pressures in Turkey. Archbishop Makarios did take several small steps in October to ease tensions on the Island, particularly the release of Mr. Denktash. Given the existing situation, much more by way of concessions from the Archbishop seemed unlikely. The Greek régime, on the other hand, appeared particularly vulnerable.

The Turkish Government wanted some clear-cut action by Greece that would acknowledge the continued vitality of the 1960 Accords. To achieve that goal, Turkey could again use its

[28] For reports of the talks, see *N.Y. Times*, 11 Sept. 1967, p. 1, col. 4; id. 13 Sept. 1967, p. 46, col. 2 (editorial).

most powerful weapon: the threat of force under Article IV of the
Treaty of Guarantee. Turkish representatives had consistently
maintained that unilateral military action was authorized by the
terms of that provision and was consistent with the United Nations
Charter. They claimed that Turkey had refrained from intervening since August 1964 in large measure beause of the presence
of the United Nations Peacekeeping Force on the Island. But
they stressed that the force must be not only *operational* but also
effective in carrying out its mandate.[29]

At the same time, the threat of force is a wasting asset unless
exercised, as we have seen. More than three years had passed
since August 1964. (And Article IV was not then used as the legal
basis for the Turkish bombing.) In the interim, the continued
drift of the crisis without solution weakened the credibility of
Turkish military threats to force a new settlement based on a
revision of the 1960 Accords acceptable to all the parties.

The presence of some 10,000 Greek troops on the Island in violation of the Treaty of Alliance provided a perfect issue for Turkey
to focus its demand for a reaffirmation of the terms of the 1960
Accords. The primary purpose of the treaty was to protect the
Island from external attack. To further that purpose, the treaty
called for a Tripartite Headquarters with 950 Greek troops and
650 Turkish troops. Their stated *raison d'être* was to 'provide for the
training of the army of the Republic of Cyprus'.[30] In fact, however, Greek troops dominated the Cypriot armed forces. Cypriot
National Guardsmen had begun wearing Greek army badges,
and new Cypriot recruits took an oath of allegiance to the Greek
king.[31] Of all the issues connected with the 1960 Accords, this was
the one on which Greece could expect the least international
support. Reports by the United Nations Secretary-General had
pointed to the presence of the Greek (and much smaller numbers
of Turkish) troops as a major source of friction on Cyprus, and
the Soviet Union in particular had repeatedly urged that they be
withdrawn. Removal of foreign troops in excess of the authorized
contingents could not only mean a reaffirmation of the 1960
Accords, it could also directly affect affairs on the Island, thus
reasserting Turkey's involvement in those affairs. It would cer-

[29] See, e.g., Letter From the Prime Minister of Turkey to the President of
the Security Council, 10 Aug. 1964, in U.N. Doc. No. S/5875, at 2 (1964).
[30] Treaty of Alliance, Art. IV.
[31] See U.N. Doc. No. S/7969, at 14 (1967).

tainly make the Island more vulnerable to the threat of a future
Turkish attack. At the same time, the decision would primarily
be Greece's, not the Archbishop's. The chances for him to scuttle
this step, as compared to other possible arrangements, would be
minimal.

This analysis is not meant to imply that the Turkish leaders had
definitely decided to bring the issue of excess Greek troops to a
head before November 1967. It is more likely they had determined that if a new crisis were triggered by attacks against Turkish Cypriots, this issue would be the focus of the Turkish response.
As was true in the discussion of other decisions, lack of published
reports makes it difficult to do more than speculate. But the issue
was so well suited to achieve the broader Turkish aims that it was
probably carefully considered in the weeks after the September
summit talks collapsed.

In all events, the National Guard attack on Turkish enclaves in
November was a catalyst for all the pent-up pressures in Turkey
for action. One journalist on the scene concluded that General
Grivas ordered the attack with the approval of the Greek Government to 'put the Turkish Cypriots in their place . . .'[32] Whether
or not that judgement is accurate, there seems little doubt from
the Secretary-General's reports that the Greek forces in Cyprus
had carefully planned the move. 'Rarely has there been a Cypriot
crisis in which—in terms solely of its immediate causes—guilt
has belonged so much to one side', _The Economist_ reported.[33]
'It is hard to escape the conclusion that the Greeks decided the
time had come not merely to show the flag but to show who is
top dog . . .'

Not only was the attack part of a premeditated design, it was in
direct defiance of the United Nations Force on the Island. It
appeared the clearest case of an action in violation of the Security
Council's injunction 'to refrain from any action or threat of action likely to worsen the situation in Cyprus or endanger international peace'. We have already analysed the argument under
Article IV that a limited Turkish use of force aimed solely at
protecting Turkish Cypriots and, therefore, at restoring the
'state of affairs' under the 1960 Accords, would be consistent
with both the pre-emptive authority of the Council and the

---

[32] _The Times_ (London), 29 Nov. 1967, p. 9, col. 8.
[33] _The Economist_, 2 Dec. 1967, p. 943, cols. 1–2.

maintenance of international peace. The situation on 15 November appeared a case in point.

On the evening of the 15th, while the fighting was still going on, the Turkish Minister of Foreign Affairs called on the United Nations Force to bring about a 'cease-fire immediately'.[34] After an all-night session, the Turkish cabinet warned on the morning of the 16th that Turkey would intervene militarily if the shooting continued.[35] That day the Cypriot Police again sent a patrol over the critical route, and on the 17th the Turkish Parliament authorized the Government 'to send troops abroad'.[36]

By the end of the day on the 17th, the United Nations Force had been successful in achieving a ceasefire and the National Guard troops had withdrawn from the besieged area (although sporadic fighting broke out again the next day). But the Turkish Government had already decided that it would insist on a good deal more than a ceasefire. In a formal note to the Greek Government,[37] Turkey demanded:

(1) Removal of the Greek soldiers on the Island in violation of the Treaty of Alliance;
(2) Removal of General Grivas;
(3) Disbandment of the entire National Guard;
(4) Disengagement in the area where the fighting took place;
(5) Authorization for Turkish Cypriots to form their own local governments and police forces in their enclaves;
(6) Compensation to Turkish Cypriots for losses resulting from the attacks; and
(7) Enlargement of the United Nations Peacekeeping Force to preclude a repetition of the attacks.

The demands were made to the Greek Government, not to the Archbishop, and it was clear from this point on that Turkey was primarily insisting on action by Greece. As reported in *The Times* (London), 'the more nationalistic spirits in the Turkish Government, as atrocity stories multiplied, decided that they had now a heaven-sent chance to settle the Cyprus issue once and for all against a weak and internationally unpopular Greek régime'.[38]

[34] Quoted in U.N. Doc. No. S/8248, at 7 (1967).
[35] *N.Y. Times*, 17 Nov. 1967, p. 6, col. 1.
[36] Id., 18 Nov. 1967, p. 3, col. 3.
[37] See Adams and Cottrell, *Cyprus Between East and West* 71 (1968).
[38] *The Times* (London), 29 Nov. 1967, p. 9, col. 8.

Several of the demands could be accomplished only by the Cypriot Government—disbandment of the National Guard, and Turkish Cypriot autonomy in the enclaves. Others would require at least the Archbishop's co-operation—disengagement, compensation, and (most important) enlargement of the United Nations Force. These were all important issues through the next seven days of international negotiations. But the key issue was the withdrawal of Greek troops. As the Turkish representative to the United Nations stated:

. . . the Turkish Government firmly believes that the only element which threatens the peace on the Island, which poses the greatest danger to the security of life of the Turkish community, and the most direct impediment to the effective functioning of UNFICYP in Cyprus, emerges as the presence of the illegal Greek Army of occupation which has been brought to the Island surreptititiously and with the collusion of the Greek Cypriot Administration.[39]

Of the other demands, no doubt the most significant were enlargement of the United Nations Force and a strengthening of its mandate. But these steps, as the Security Council debates had made clear, would require the Cypriot Government's approval, and the Archbishop had frequently stated that he would not sanction such measures except as part of a much larger settlement package.

The Greek Government readily agreed to recall General Grivas, purportedly on a temporary basis, in order 'to be fully informed of the situation'.[40] He had apparently been an embarrassment for some time, and the ability of the Greek leaders and the Archbishop to control his actions was questionable. Withdrawal of the Greek forces, however, was a much more important measure. On the one hand, it would signify a major step away from enosis. The several thousand Greek troops on the Island, and the various steps—real and symbolic—to integrate Greek and Greek Cypriot soldiers were the strongest tangible ties between Greece and Cyprus. If the excess Greek forces were withdrawn, the continued independence of the Island would appear more likely. On the other hand, withdrawal would also imply that the Treaty of Alliance was still valid and, therefore,

[39] 22 U.N. SCOR, 1383d meeting 4 (1967).
[40] 22 U.N. SCPR, 1383d meeting 27 (1967). Interestingly, the quoted reason for recalling General Grivas is not included in the official text of the Security Council debates. See 22 U.N. SCOR, 1383d meeting 4 (1967).

that the 1960 Accords would be the starting point for negotiating any new settlement.

B. PRESSURES FROM THE GREEK CYPRIOTS

We have seen that the Archbishop had become increasingly disenchanted with the Greek Government and probably with the prospect of enosis as well. The possibility of rule by a military dictatorship could not have been an appealing one, quite apart from the economic considerations that favoured continued independence. At the same time, any step that might seem to endorse the 1960 Accords could undermine the Archbishop's campaign to cut free from those agreements.

With respect to the Treaty of Alliance, the problem was particularly difficult because the Cypriot Government had formally declared that the Treaty had been terminated as a result of alleged violations of its terms by Turkey.[41] Immediately after fighting broke out in December 1963, the Turkish contingent moved out of its barracks and took up positions on the Nicosia–Kyrenia road. According to a Turkish representative, this move was made because the contingent 'considered it extremely dangerous for its own security to remain in its barracks which were situated in an area controlled by the Greek Cypriot terrorists, and was forced to move on to a new garrison in a more secure sector of the Nicosia area'.[42] One observer has claimed that the real reason for the move was to protect the road to several Turkish Cypriot positions.[43]

The Treaty of Alliance does not state where the Turkish and Greek contingents are to be stationed. At the time the Treaty was signed, however, a supplementary agreement was also concluded 'for the application of the Treaty of Alliance'. That agreement provides that 'the Hellenic and Turkish Forces shall be garrisoned in the same area as near each other as possible and within a radius of five miles . . .'[44] It appears unquestioned by the Cypriot Government that the Turkish contingent stationed in Nicosia met those conditions.

[41] e.g., 19 U.N. SCOR, 1136th meeting 38 (1964).
[42] 19 U.N. SCOR, 1136th meeting 9 (1964).
[43] Foley, *Legacy of Strife* 170 (1964).
[44] Agreement Between the Kingdom of Greece, the Republic of Turkey and the Republic of Cyprus for the Application of the Treaty of Alliance, 16 Aug. 1960, Art. XV.

The Cypriot Government claimed, however, that the deployment of the Turkish troops outside their stations in occupation of sovereign Cypriot territory violated the treaty. Two days after the United Nations Force was established, Archbishop Makarios wrote to the Turkish Foreign Minister demanding that the troops return to their barracks. When Turkey rejected the demand, the Archbishop declared that the Republic of Cyprus considered the treaty terminated as a result of a material breach by Turkey.[45]

At first it appeared that the Cypriot allegation was based on a decision in 1961 by a Committee of Foreign Ministers established under the treaty: 'the present camps of the Greek and Turkish contingents should be considered as their permanent camp unless and until decided otherwise by the Committee of Ministers'.[46] On the basis of that decision, the Cypriot Government contended that '[t]he continued presence . . . of the Turkish contingent [away from its permanent camp] constitutes a violation of the territorial integrity of the Republic of Cyprus' and that this violation justified Cypriot renunciation of the treaty.[47] This argument is obviously vulnerable, however, since the Ministers' decision was not part of the treaty and circumstances had changed markedly from 1961 to 1964.

Subsequently, Cypriot legal advisers focused their arguments on the basic purpose of the treaty—to 'provide for the training of the army of the Republic of Cyprus'. The officials claimed that a Cypriot army was needed only to protect against an external attack. The Greek and Turkish troops—on the Island to train that army—were, therefore, not authorized to leave their permanent positions except in the event of such an attack, and then only on the orders of the Tripartite Headquarters.

Turkish representatives did not rebut these Cypriot assertions, except to reject summarily any renunciation of the treaty. Turkey could have argued that the parties to the Treaty of Alliance intended that troops of any of the three Guarantor Powers could be used unilaterally when necessary to re-establish 'the state of affairs' as was the situation after Christmas Day, 1963.

---

[45] See U.N. Doc. No. S/5647 (1964); U.N. Doc. No. S/5636 (1964). For the Turkish response, see U.N. Doc. No. S/5663 (1964).

[46] Decision of the Committee of Ministers of the Treaty of Alliance, 28 June 1961, quoted in 19 U.N. SCOR, 1136th meeting 38 (1964).

[47] Id. at 38–9.

Except for general Soviet and Czech references to violations of Cypriot sovereignty by the presence of foreign troops under 'unequal' treaties, no other country publicly supported the Cypriot view. But the Cypriot Government consistently maintained its position that the Treaty of Alliance had been terminated.

As a result, the Cypriot Government was bound to resist a Greek troop withdrawal that was rooted in the provisions of the Treaty of Alliance. Yet that was precisely the legal basis on which Turkey founded its demand. If it were possible for Cyprus to secure the removal of *all* Greek and Turkish troops—not just those in excess of the treaty contingents—the problem would be minimized, but it was apparent from the outset that Turkey would not agree to that arrangement. On the other hand, apart from the rationale for withdrawal, the possible departure of Greek troops from the Island had advantages for the Cypriot Government. Assuming the Archbishop had concluded that enosis was either infeasible or undesirable, or both, removal of the troops would free the Island from a substantial restraint on the Greek Cypriots' freedom of action. Moreover, the Archbishop was apparently seriously concerned, even after the failure of the Greek–Turkish summit talks, that Greece might accede to Turkish pressures for partition. Just as in the 1950s, all the arguments for enosis, or for the right of Greek Cypriots to choose union, could be turned in favour of some territorial concessions to Turkey, or of the right of Turkish Cypriots to choose that course.

On this basis, it seems reasonable to speculate that the Archbishop did not exert pressures on Greek leaders to keep their troops in Cyprus. He may even have urged withdrawal, although he could not afford to state publicly his support for the step. It is also probable that the Archbishop wanted the removal linked to a Turkish promise not to intervene militarily in the future and a general renunciation of Turkey's alleged rights under Article IV of the Treaty of Guarantee. The main advantage of Greek troops to the Cypriot Government was that they could help to deter or defend against a Turkish invasion. If the danger was eliminated, troop withdrawals could lead to substantial gains for the Cypriot Government. Even though the invasion threat continued, the Archbishop probably did not oppose withdrawal if, but only if, some mechanism could be found to avoid the appearance of acceding to a Turkish ultimatum. The question, then, was how to devise that mechanism.

C. PRESSURES BY THE UNITED STATES AND OTHER NATO NATIONS

The interests of the United States and its NATO allies in the 1967 affair were much like their interests in prior problems in the crisis: to restore peace to the Island in the short run, to promote a new settlement in the long run, and above all to avoid war between Greece and Turkey. But United States mediation efforts in 1964 had not only weakened American influence in Turkey, they had also impaired United States prestige in Greece. America had meddled in the crisis, and though this meddling may have saved Cyprus from an invasion, Greece wanted clear support for Cypriot 'self-determination'. But the United States refused to comply. In 1964, the Greek prime minister had accused the United States of being pro-Turkish, anti-American demonstrations were held in the streets of Athens, and the Greek press flailed President Johnson for his efforts in the dispute.[48]

These problems were partially offset as a result of the Greek military *coup*. For the first time in two decades, the Greek press was under the complete control of a government willing to muzzle any criticism of its actions. More important, Greek military strength was largely dependent on United States aid. That aid was sharply curtailed immediately after the *coup*, and still had not been fully restored at the time of the November blow-up.

On 22 November, the United States chose to join with England and Canada in proposing a settlement formula. The Canadian prime minister, Pearson, was selected to make the proposal. In essence, it provided that:

(1) Greek and Turkish troop strengths would be reduced to the Treaty of Alliance levels;
(2) the United Nations Force would be enlarged;
(3) Turkish Cypriots who suffered losses in the attacks would be compensated and the future security of the Turkish Cypriot areas assured; and
(4) Turkey would guarantee not to intervene militarily in the future.[49]

[48] See *N.Y. Times*, 1 Mar. 1964, p. 1, col. 1, p. 3, col. 1; id., 4 Mar. 1964, p. 10, cols. 4, 7; id., 27 Feb. 1964, p. 10, cols. 3, 4.
[49] See *The Times* (London) 24 Nov. 1967, p. 5, col. 6.

This package proposal contained some concessions and some gains for Cyprus, for Greece, and for Turkey. But the responses from all three Governments were sufficiently far apart that substantial negotiating efforts would be needed.[50] Yet the situation was so volatile that it was impossible to bring representatives of the three nations together at the same table. (Indeed, that had not once occurred in the previous four years.) Turkey reiterated its demand for the withdrawal of all Greek troops in excess of the authorized contingents, refused to discuss the situation with Greece until the withdrawal, and threatened an invasion within a few days to establish military parity with the Greek forces unless Turkish demands were met. Greek leaders on their part were willing to consult on the crisis with Turkish representatives, but rejected the Turkish 'no discussion without withdrawal' position, insisting instead on 'no withdrawal without discussion'. In particular, some formula would have to be found to avoid the humiliating appearance of succumbing to a Turkish threat. In these circumstances, third-party mediation efforts were essential.

On 22 November, the same day as Mr. Pearson's abortive appeal, President Johnson appointed former Deputy Secretary of Defense Cyrus Vance as special envoy to help in mediating the dispute. Also on that day the United Nations Secretary-General appointed as his special representative in the crisis his Under-Secretary for Special Political Affairs, Jose Rolz-Bennett. Two days later, Athens and Ankara accepted a third mediator, Manlio Brosio, the Secretary-General of NATO. Mr. Vance concentrated his efforts on Athens and Ankara while Mr. Rolz-Bennett focused on Nicosia. Mr. Brosio provided further support in trying to bring the two NATO nations to an agreement.

Mr. Vance began in the classic mode of a mediator between two nations on the brink of war; he first sought time to manoeuvre. After gaining a Turkish commitment to delay an invasion for at least a few days, he conferred alternately with Greek and Turkish representatives. The official United States position was that he acted only as an intermediary, and that he did not threaten sanctions against either nation.[51] But there were some reports that the United States might cut off military aid to both sides as it did during the 1965 India–Pakistan war.[52] Even if Mr. Vance did not

---

[50] See *N.Y. Times*, 23 Nov. p. 1, col. 6; id., 24 Nov. 1967, p. 1, col. 8.

[51] Id., 23 Nov. 1967, p. 13, col. 1.

[52] See id., 24 Nov. 1967, p. 18, col. 5.

directly discuss future military assistance for Greece and Turkey, the issue must have been very much in the minds of leaders in those countries, for both depended on American assistance to maintain their armed forces. The United States was in a particularly good position to influence Greek policy. Although relations between the two nations had been seriously strained by the April *coup*, they might be improved by a significant act of Greek statesmanship. In more practical terms, Greece would have little chance in a war with Turkey unless the United States intervened.

Mr. Vance collaborated in his efforts with both Mr. Brosio and Mr. Rolz-Bennett. On a single day, 26 November, for example, one was in Ankara, one in Athens, and one in Nicosia.[53] Slowly a plan was developed between Greece and Turkey, with Mr. Vance acting as principal mediator. The key step was the Greek Government's agreement, reportedly on the 24th, to withdraw its excess troops if some procedural formula could be found to avoid the appearance of a complete capitulation to Turkey. Major substantive issues remained, however, and the Turkish press and public opinion were calling for war. As to the troops themselves, the Greek régime apparently wanted a lengthy timetable for withdrawal, but Turkey insisted on quick action. Further, the Archbishop called for the complete withdrawal of all Greek and Turkish troops, which would have avoided the appearance of a return to the 1960 Accords. As for the other Turkish demands, the security arrangements for Turkish Cypriots were the most important. The technique apparently used by Mr. Vance and the other mediators was to press Greece and Turkey to some settlement, and then to put the Archbishop in the position of either accepting the settlement or being the isolated cause of a continuing crisis that threatened to explode at any moment. On 30 November, Greece and Turkey finally reached an agreement.[54]

D. THE DECISION

The military and diplomatic pressures on the Greek Government to reach an agreement on troop withdrawals are clear enough. First, and most important, was the imminent threat of a Turkish invasion backed up by superior military power. Further,

[53] See id., 27 Nov. 1967, p. 3, col. 2.
[54] Id., 1 Dec. 1967, p. 1, col. 2.

the United States had probably indicated that it would not intervene militarily to prevent a Turkish invasion. Second, the Greek régime was in an uncomfortably isolated position in the international community and was eager to take some step to help extricate itself. Third, the crisis had been triggered by a premeditated Greek attack, led by a Greek General, in violation of Security Council resolutions and arrangements with the United Nations Force commander. These pressures combined with the fact that the excess Greek troops were on the Island in violation of the Treaty of Alliance. There was general agreement, at least in the Security Council, that renegotiation by all the parties was the proper way to revise the conditions established by the 1960 Accords. Finally, on the domestic side, the Greek Government's control of the press minimized the dangers of an aroused Greek public.

The Greek–Turkish settlement agreement provided for withdrawing of all their forces in excess of the authorized contingents within 45 to 90 days, disbanding the Greek National Guard, scaling down the Cypriot police force, and enlarging the United Nations Force. The agreement, however, still had to be made public in a face-saving way acceptable to Greece; otherwise there would be no settlement. Some scheme would have to be developed for the Greek decision to become an act of international statesmanship rather than of national appeasement. This was essential to make the agreement palatable not only to Greek leaders but to Archbishop Makarios as well. In that task, the United Nations Secretary-General played a critical role.

On 24 November Greece and Turkey arranged that any agreement between them would take the form of an appeal by the Secretary-General that they and Cyprus could accept. The stage had already been set for this procedure by an initial appeal two days earlier from Mr. Thant calling on all the parties to exercise the utmost restraint and announcing the appointment of his personal representative.[55]

Some reports have indicated that Mr. Vance developed the formula 'to provide the weaker side with a ladder it can climb down . . .'[56] On the other hand, Mr. Thant stated that he acted independently of the United States mediator.[57] In all events, the

[55] See U.N. Doc. No. S/8248/Add. 3 (1967).
[56] *The Economist*, 15 Dec. 1967, p. 1031, col. 1.
[57] *N.Y. Times*, 5 Dec. 1967, p. 2, col. 4.

Secretary-General's second appeal was issued on the 24th.[58] It urged all three Governments 'to work out a programme for the phased reduction looking toward ultimate complete withdrawal' of 'all non-Cypriot' armed forces. So phrased, the appeal made a concession to the Greek Cypriot position in not excluding the authorized contingents. At the same time, it stressed that the withdrawal should be 'phased' and should be part of a long-range plan for 'the positive demilitarization of Cyprus . . .' These qualifiers left ample room for maintaining the Greek and Turkish contingents.

The Secretary-General's second appeal also pressed all the parties to act in accordance with their Charter obligations and, therefore, to 'desist from the use of force or the threat of the use of force . . . [and] refrain from any military intervention' in Cyprus. This plea, of course, was directed squarely at Turkey, and was also designed to gain support from the Cypriot Government. The Security Council met through most of the night on the 24th, hearing bitter exchanges between Greece, Turkey, and Cyprus, and finally adopting a 'consensus' that noted 'with satisfaction' the Secretary-General's efforts.[59]

When Greece and Turkey finally concluded their agreement on 30 November, it appeared for a time that the crisis was over— that the Secretary-General would issue a new appeal embodying the terms of the agreement and that the parties involved would accept it. But, as might have been expected, the Archbishop was adamant in resisting a reduction in Cypriot security forces or an increase in the United Nations Force except as part of a larger arrangement for United Nations guarantees of Cypriot safety and independence. In the next few days Turkish leaders grew increasingly impatient at the delay. Finally, after another intense round of negotiations—again with Mr. Vance acting as principal mediator—the Secretary-General did issue a third appeal.[60] In the interim, Greece and Turkey had apparently decided to make public their agreement in spite of the Archbishop's failure to accept it. Perhaps they thought this would increase the international pressure on the Cypriot Government, perhaps Turkey had demanded some public acknowledgement of the deal. In all

[58] U.N. Doc. No. S/8248/Add. 5 (1967).

[59] See 22 U.N. SCOR, 1383d meeting 14 (1967).

[60] U.N. Doc. No. S/8248/Add. 6 (1967). This document also includes the responses of the Cypriot, Greek, and Turkish Governments.

events, the Secretary-General wrote: 'Particularly do I appeal to the Governments of Greece and Turkey . . . to carry out an expeditious withdrawal of those of their forces in excess of their respective contingents in Cyprus.' He added that, 'with regard to any further role that it might be considered desirable for UNFICYP to undertake, I gather that this could involve, subject to the necessary action by the Security Council, enlarging the mandate of the Force so as to give it broader functions . . . My good offices in connection with such matters would, of course, be available to the parties on request.'

The Greek Government had already been preparing the Greek people for the withdrawal by ordering the nation's newspapers to stress the Secretary-General's prior appeals; it did the same in this case. The Greek Government responded on the same day the third appeal was issued. The response was a one-sentence letter taking note of the appeal 'which we accept and which we are ready to carry out expeditiously'. The Turkish Government also accepted the appeal on 3 December. Its reply was somewhat longer and included a specific affirmation of Turkey's rights under the 1960 Accords. The Cypriot Government delayed a day in answering, but then—presumably under further pressure by all the parties—accepted withdrawal of the excess Greek and Turkish troops, characterizing it as a step 'toward the ultimate and complete withdrawal from the Republic of Cyprus of all non-Cypriot armed forces other than those of the United Nations'. The Cypriot note indicated, however, that further measures, including expansion of the role of United Nations Force, would have to be considered in the context of international guarantees against external attack. A subsequent speech by the Cypriot Foreign Minister made it clear that any revisions in internal security arrangements must be part of a broader settlement in the framework of full demilitarization.[61] Finally, the Cypriot representative to the United Nations stressed that 'we shall not now consent to any bilateral effort between Greece and Turkey with regard to the Cyprus problem'.[62]

On 8 December the first Greek troops sailed for Athens; the withdrawal took place quietly and without incident. On the Turkish side, the invasion force was disbanded. The Security Council met again on 20 and 22 December, but could agree on

[61] See *N.Y. Times*, 5 Dec. 1967, p. 2, col. 6.
[62] 21 U.N. SCPR, 1385th meeting 22 (1967).

no more than another extension of the existing mandate of the United Nations Peacekeeping Force.[63]

Withdrawal of Greek troops from Cyprus probably averted a military disaster for Greece. It may have also reflected a fundamental decision by the Greek régime to disengage from the affairs of the Island. There is some evidence that the Turkish Government may be similarly inclined. Both are no doubt wary of being swung by the tail by their respective communities on Cyprus. Both may have concluded that only those communities can settle the Island's affairs.

[63] See 21 U.N. SCOR, 1386th meeting 1–2, 4 (1967). The Soviet and French positions on the Charter limitations concerning peacekeeping operations obviously have had an important effect throughout the crisis on efforts to enlarge the force's mandate.

VI

SOME CONCLUDING COMMENTS

THIS study began with a disclaimer to aspirations of quantitative analysis concerning the impact of law on the four national decisions discussed. Each decision was examined in an effort to isolate the ways in which law was involved or, absent records, in which such involvement appeared probable. From this analysis a picture has emerged of 'how' law related to the decisions, though 'how much' remains uncertain.

It is worth re-emphasizing that this focus has inevitably distorted the history of Cyprus in the 1950s and 1960s. The four decisions were all critical to that history, but they were not the only critical decisions. The various national reactions to the 1965 report of the United Nations mediator, Mr. Galo Plaza, for example, received only passing reference, though the report was a key element in the crisis as a whole. Further, non-legal elements in each decision were given less attention than would emerge in a more balanced analysis. The personality and background of Archbishop Makarios, for example, is obviously significant in considering the Greek Cypriot decision in 1963; the personality and background of the other national leaders may be no less relevant in examining the British, Greek, and Turkish decisions. Also, at many junctures in each decision-making process, internal politics were a major factor that affected Cyprus and the other parties to the controversy. In 1967, for example, both the Turkish ultimatums and the Greek responses can be attributed in part to the international unpopularity of the Greek military régime.

It is by no means clear that any of the decisions would have been made differently if legal considerations had been ignored. Each reveals a different dominant aspect of the relevance of law to national decision-making in international affairs.

In the mid-1950s, the objectives of British policy toward Cyprus were conceived and articulated in terms of two principles of international law: the immutability of sovereignty and the sanctity of treaties. Those principles were tools for communicating policies to others and for legitimizing the consequences of following those policies. But the role of law in the 1958 decision went beyond advocacy. The two principles seemed to take on a life of their own in the formulation of British policy. They impeded the search for a long-run solution compatible with the interests of all the parties. Discounting the rhetoric inevitable in speech-making, reiteration of those principles appeared as a substitute for thought and negotiation. Yet manipulations of the British legal position ultimately undercut the strength of that position. The main Greek legal argument in the General Assembly from 1950 to 1956 was grounded on the principle of self-determination, which the Greek and Cypriot leaders thought could only lead to enosis. The initial response of the United Kingdom was defensive—based primarily on Article 2(7) of the United Nations Charter. British officials later took the offensive and, by suggesting partition, sought to turn the self-determination argument against Greece. Britain successfully positioned Turkey as a countervailing force against Greek pressures for enosis, leaving England as a mediating middleman. But the situation was inherently unstable, for partition was an unsatisfactory solution to most Cypriots. Yet the very fact that partition was suggested by England cast doubt on the need for continued British rule. England had successfully countered the Greek legal case at the cost of her own sovereignty over Cyprus.

In the decision of Archbishop Makarios to propose revisions of the Cypriot Constitution, a range of alternatives was available to remedy the breakdown of the Island's internal legal structure. The Archbishop chose the one that would deal with the immediate problem and yet minimize the chances of international opposition. Of all the 1960 Accords, revision of the Constitution was least susceptible to attack on the ground that agreement by all the parties was essential. An appeal for renegotiation, rather than an announcement of abrogation, further undercut the charge of unilateral revision. Greece in particular, although sympathetic to the Archbishop's claim that the Cypriot Constitution was not working, probably urged that the Accords be revised rather than abrogated, and perhaps also that the matter be brought to the United Nations. That organization could not be expected to force revision, but at least in the long run it was likely to provide support for renegotiation. And in terms of the Cypriot Government's arguments within the Security Council, its representatives viewed their decision as involving essentially legal issues.

In Turkey's response to the August 1964 attacks on Turkish Cypriot villages, the Turkish Government's prior reliance on Article IV of the Treaty of Guarantee imposed limitations on its ability to resolve the crisis with force. Unilateral action under Article IV requires prior consultations with other Guarantor Powers and is restricted to 're-establishing the state of affairs created by the present Treaty'. There is room for argument concerning the meaning of the treaty's provisions as well as their consistency with the obligations imposed by the United Nations Charter. But the very framing of the questions in these terms provided a legal structure for considering the controversy. Further, it reduced the risk that any armed intervention by Turkey would serve as a precedent for military action by Turkey or by other countries in affairs other than the Cyprus situation. The circumstances that produced the Treaty of Guarantee may arise elsewhere, but this appears unlikely. Ultimately, Turkish representatives turned to the inherent right of self-defence to support the decision to use force. That theory allowed, at least in Turkish eyes, more flexibility than Article IV of the Treaty of Guarantee. But it too imposed at least some restraint on Turkish military action.

The pressures of the international legal system in the August 1964 situation failed in the sense that they did not stop the unilateral use of force by Turkey. Those pressures did play a substantial role, however, in limiting the likelihood that earlier threats would be carried out. Further, in the early months of the crisis, the very strength of the case that the Treaty of Guarantee authorizes unilateral intervention under certain circumstances may have helped to deter Archbishop Makarios from putting down all Turkish Cypriot resistance. But, by August 1964, the credibility of the threat had apparently run out.

Finally, the 1967 decision of the Greek Government is perhaps the most difficult to analyse from a legal perspective. In a sense, the whole incident can be characterized as a threat to use force by one country and a capitulation by the threatened nation to avoid war and almost certain defeat. Turkey did not achieve all its demands, but Greece did accede to the key one.

In another sense, however, more was involved. In terms of our particular concern with the role of law, the issue of troop withdrawal was framed by Turkey as a question of enforcing the 1960 Accords. The Turkish Government wanted Greece to take some step to affirm the continuing validity of the Accords. In this sense, law was a catalyst for the decision. Further, Greece was able to reach a solution that averted war in large measure because of the efforts of the three mediators and, most important, the focal position of the Secretary-General. More than at any other time in the entire Cyprus dispute, the United Nations provided a neutral peacemaker to which all the parties could respond without impairing national prestige. Neither legal norms nor legal institutions stopped Turkey from being stronger than Greece or from exercising its muscle. They did, however, provide a means to check the stronger nation from constantly raising its demands and to allow the weaker country to extricte itself with some self-esteem. They offered an acceptable way to lose. They did not prevent the threat of war, but they did have a role in preventing the outbreak of war.

Viewing the four decisions as a whole, therefore, the relevance of law emerges in several quite distinct ways. First, law was involved in the formulation of each issue for decision. The 1958 British decision to renounce sovereignty over the Island, for example, was a decision to relinquish rights established under the international law. The decision had other dimensions: Britain's strategic interests no longer required complete control over the Island; the results of maintaining such control were not worth the cost. But the strength of the case in law for continued British dominion was a critical element in British policy formulation.

Second, a restraining function was another aspect of the role of law. In 1963, for example, the Makarios Government apparently wanted to abrogate the entire set of Accords negotiated at Zurich and London. But the Archbishop chose instead to propose revisions of only one of those agreements, the Constitution. Revision avoided the legal case against unilateral abrogation. Of all the Accords, the Constitution seemed most persuasively a matter of Cypriot concern. In the 1963 decision, therefore, domestic legal considerations were an impetus for decision and international legal constraints structured its outcome.

Third, the function of law in framing issues for decision goes beyond restraint; it also involves channelling the authorization and exercise of power. A legal case under Article IV of the Treaty of Guarantee was critical to establishing the circumstances in which unilateral intervention by Turkey was justified. Article IV restrained Turkey by establishing a set of prerequisites for such intervention. But much more important, at least in Turkish eyes, the provision authorized military action if that action was necessary to restore the *status quo* established by the 1960 Accords. As one of the Guarantor Powers, Turkey was charged with unilateral as well as collective responsibility for maintaining that state of affairs. Law thus channelled the process of decision in 1964; it had a similar impact in the other decisions.

Fourth, in each of the decisions, law provided a tool of advocacy for policy-makers. Representatives of all the nations involved made extensive appeals to legal principles, particularly in the United Nations, to enlist the support of other countries. Those appeals were directed at the maintenance of treaty obligations in the case of Britain in the 1950s and Turkey in the 1960s, and at norms that allegedly overrode those obligations in the case of the other parties. How important were those appeals? At the least, the parties apparently thought they were significant. With the exception of Great Britain, none of the parties was a major power. Greece and Turkey both depended on the United States for military assistance and the Greek Cypriots used Soviet and East European arms. Beyond this factor, Greece, Turkey, and Cyprus were all vulnerable to collective international pressures, particularly through the United Nations. Each articulated the legal basis for its position in debates before the Security Council and the General Assembly. The framing of issues in legal terms implied a series of procedural and substantive limits on their consideration. Recognition of those limits, in turn, meant that the role of law went beyond the preparation of briefs for actions already decided; it was a central element in the decisions themselves. The continued validity of the 1960 Accords, for example, was a key objective in Turkish policy throughout the 1967 crisis, and the basis for much of the pressure brought to bear on Greece by the Turkish Government. Formulation of the objective was repeatedly made in legal terms and defended by essentially legal analysis.

Fifth, international institutions—creatures and creators of law—also had substantial roles in each of the decisions. The United Nations was obviously the most important. Among the most apparent manifestations of legal considerations throughout the entire crisis were in the United Nations debates that continued through the 1950s, particularly in the General Assembly, and the 1960s, particularly in the Security Council. In 1964 alone, the Security Council considered Cyprus at 27 separate meetings; by the end of 1965, it had passed 10 resolutions concerning the crisis. The Council debates revealed a display of emotion by opposing parties rarely on view in those chambers of diplomacy. Almost every meeting began with a procedural wrangle that sometimes took several hours to resolve. These controversies must have been as irritating to observers as they are to readers. At the same time, they may have been necessary preludes to substantive action. One has the feeling when reading the debates that mistrust and bitterness were so deep that no resolution of substantive problems was possible without some initial cooling-off period during which emotions could be controlled through discussion of seemingly trivial matters. In these circumstances some mechanism was necessary to maintain discussion while an atmosphere for possible compromise slowly developed. In the main, this mechanism was conflict concerning the Council's *modus operandi*. And it worked remarkably well. By providing predictability through precedent, law frequently enables people to perceive an incident as part of a pattern rather than as unique; and consequently increases their willingness to accept the outcome. On substantive issues, the phenomenon is less common in international than domestic affairs. But in a whole range of procedural contexts, particularly in the United Nations, this function was critical.

The United Nations was, of course, involved in the decisions in ways more significant than as a forum in which each party could publicize its wrath at the others while some agreement, at least temporary and partial, could be negotiated. Most important, the organization both raised and focused the costs of the unilateral use of force. Time has not been a particularly successful healer on Cyprus, but by checking the renewal of violence and by allowing time to lessen the risks of a new explosion, the United Nations may have averted decisions that would have more seriously endangered world peace. There have been sporadic outbreaks of violence since 1964, but the United Nations Peacekeeping Force has kept them to a minimum. Creation of the force marked the first time that all five permanent members of the Council unanimously voted to set up a peacekeeping army. Both the United States and the Soviet Union were deeply concerned with the crisis, and both concluded that maintenance of peace on the Island would further their interests in comparison with the possible alternatives. The crisis presented a test case, therefore, for the effectiveness of United Nations peacekeeping machinery. The results to date are mixed, but on balance the machinery has been successful.

Viewed as a whole, the crisis has illustrated the broad range of mechanisms for peaceful settlement available under the aegis of the United Nations. As soon as the Security Council became seized of the dispute, it took on a variety of new international dimensions; and an implicit set of restraints on the renewal of violence was brought into play. The General Assembly debates, although mentioned only briefly in this analysis, also had a significant impact, particularly in terms of the comparative positions of Cyprus and Turkey. Further, the crisis involved intensive mediation efforts by Mr. Galo Plaza, acting under the Security Council's resolution of 4 March 1964. His efforts did not succeed in settling the differences between the two communities on the Island or between the other parties involved, but he did narrow and focus those differences. Finally, the good offices of the Secretary-General were utilized on numerous occasions, particularly in the 1967 affair, to avert imminent explosion. The Governments of Cyprus, Greece, and Turkey were all able to respond to the Secretary-General's appeals in ways that would have otherwise not been possible. These United Nations attempts to contain the conflict by shaping national decisions were complemented, of course, by other arrangements outside the organization. Negotiations have been held between the Guarantor Powers, between Greece and Turkey, and more recently between representatives of the two communities on the Island. Third-party mediation procedures were also instituted by the United States. But over the course of the 1950s and especially the 1960s, the dominant, continuing efforts at peaceful settlement were within the United Nations structure.

Two other international organizations, NATO and the European Commission on Human Rights, also had significant, though less important and more specialized, roles in several of the decisions. NATO, a military arrangement, was a cohesive force binding Greece and Turkey throughout the 1950s and 1960s. The organization was particularly significant because the military was a dominant element in the governments of both countries. As a defensive alliance, NATO helped to lessen the risk of a violent clash by two of its members. It also provided a forum where Greek and Turkish officials were virtually forced to sit down together. Under the procedure adopted in 1956, both nations were committed to the peaceful resolution within NATO of any dispute between them. The absence of Cypriot representatives limited the impact of NATO in several ways, as we have seen, but that absence may also have strengthened the fragile bonds between Greece and Turkey, enabling negotiations to proceed.

The role of the European Commission on Human Rights was of a much different character. In both the 1958 and the 1967 decisions, the Commission's procedures were used to bring pressure on the decision-making government. In the first instance, Greece set the machinery in motion against Great Britain; in the second, the Commission's efforts were directed against Greece. In each situation, the government under investigation was put on the defensive because of both the Commission's independent power once it accepts a case and the adverse publicity consequences that could flow from a finding that the Convention on Human Rights had been violated.

If any single theme can be said to link the four decisions, it is the issue of treaty rights and obligations. Britain rested much of its case on the Treaty of Lausanne in the 1950s, Turkey on the Zurich–London Accords in the 1960s. There is no more fundamental principle in the liturgy of international law than that agreements among nations must be respected. Statements of the doctrine, however, often appear as affirmations of faith rather than of principle rooted in the basic structure of international law as it is practised. And one who reads the views of legal theorists from some of the developing countries has a sharp sense of the limitations on their commitment to norms, including *pacta sunt servanda*, that matured long before their nations were born. The Security Council's considerations of the Cyprus crisis in the 1960s, like those of the General Assembly in the prior decade, provide no ringing affirmation of the doctrine. Most United Nations members have concluded that the 1960 treaty structure is inadequate to meet the Island's current needs. But one gains a sense from the debates in both the Council and the Assembly that the place to begin is the existing structure. After 1967, this meant that the 1960 Accords could not be rejected solely on the ground that they are no longer satisfactory to two of the parties, just as the Treaty of Lausanne could not be terminated without the agreement of England.

Closely related is the most striking failure of the international legal system when viewing the four decisions together: the system has not succeeded in developing any ordered system of treaty revision. It may be argued that throughout the 1950s there was underway a kind of international process for the revision of the Treaty of Lausanne that ultimately led to the Zurich and London Conferences. The same may have been happening throughout the 1960s to the Accords that resulted from those Conferences. Yet those processes of treaty revision are messy and confused, if they can be called processes at all. There are no orderly procedures to oblige one party to an international agreement to accede to another party's request to sit down together and renegotiate that agreement in good faith. A persuasive case can be made that such a negotiating obligation is necessary to the whole régime of treaties as well as the fundamental United Nations purpose of maintaining the peace. The interests, attitudes, and judgements of nations inevitably change over time in response to multiple stimuli—internal and external—and if international agreements are to represent viable joint undertakings, changes in their provisions must not be permanently precluded. The more specific those provisions and the longer the term that is stipulated, the greater is the risk of an eventual breach by one of the parties unless an obligation to negotiate revisions in good faith is incorporated in the agreement.

The importance of this obligation, if it is fulfilled, should not be underestimated. The requirement of good-faith bargaining, imposed when the legal system is unwilling to prescribe the substance of the bargain, has been enormously useful in Anglo-American domestic law, and there is no reason to suggest that it would be less so in international affairs. The problem, of course, is whether the setting in which the obligation operates can exert the pressure necessary to bring the parties to act upon it. Obviously, no international version of the National Labor Relations Board of the United States is an immediate prospect. But viewing the four decisions over time, there appears an increasing sentiment among the nations not directly involved in the Cyprus crisis that the parties are under a duty to bargain in good faith. Sooner or later the parties' dependence on the co-operation of these nations in so many aspects of their international lives, if not simply a 'decent respect for the opinions of mankind', may press them to acknowledge this duty.

Reading the recent debates in the United Nations concerning the crisis, one gets a sense that most nations agree there *ought* to be, at a minimum, such an obligation imposed on the parties to the 1960 Accords. Yet no mechanism has been devised to implement it. The machinery is available in the Charter. The Security Council may recommend 'appropriate procedures or methods of adjustment', acting under Chapter VI. And it probably may make binding decisions concerning procedures of treaty revision, enforceable by appropriate sanctions, acting under Chapter VII. But it is not readily conceivable that the Security Council will use this mandatory power in the future any more than it has in the past.

In part, of course, the problem of treaty renegotiation is inherent in the difficulty of national decision-making in international affairs. In each case examined, significant pressures were brought to bear on the decision-makers from beyond their nations' borders. But the focus of decision-making was a single nation, not a group of nations. The difference is perhaps one of degree. Britain's decision in 1958 and Greece's decision a decade later were virtually forced upon them. Further, considerations of the Cyprus crisis in the Security Council indicate that, over time, its deliberations may produce both considered collective judgements and shifts in those judgements as events develop. In the seemingly endless Council debates on Cyprus one can detect, over an extended period, the development of understandings that seem to represent the workings of a corporate body and to transcend the decision-making processes of its separate member-states. None the less, these understandings have yet to be translated into specific steps toward an orderly revision of the 1960 Accords.

The problem has been accentuated by a second major failing in the international legal system: the lack of any procedures for participation of groups other than national governments in most international institutions. The problem was apparent in the analysis of England's decision in 1958; there was no international forum in which Cypriots, Greek or Turkish, had a right to be heard. As a result, both communities were forced to speak through their 'parent' countries, Greece and Turkey. The inevitable result was to distort the positions of both groups as well as to draw them closer to their spokesmen than might otherwise have happened. This in turn may have restrained them from accepting solutions that were possibly in their interests but were not acceptable to those spokesmen. Throughout the three decisions in the 1960s,

Turkish Cypriots generally appeared in the United Nations and other international institutions through their sponsor, the Turkish Government, with similarly distorting consequences. No one can say with certainty what would have happened if these weaknesses in the international legal system had been remedied. Even today, although a legal norm to support the claims of colonial peoples may be more generally accepted, no international forum exists to impose pressure on colonial powers to negotiate directly with those peoples. The underlying problem is fading with the disappearance of colonies. But the Cyprus case is a prime example of the failings of legal norms and institutions to provide a viable alternative to violence in relations between colony and ruling power.

Such failings of the international legal system have too often led to a curious joinder of judgements: international law does not exist; international law can somehow bring world peace. This study concludes that both judgements are false. Law does operate to structure national decision-making in the international arena, though it will never alone bring world peace any more than it has brought domestic peace. But its limitations should not obscure its reality.

COMMENT

Louis Henkin*

PROFESSOR Ehrlich has uncovered about as much as could be uncovered of the different parts played by international law in four decisions which he has isolated for analysis out of the recent, tangled story of Cyprus. I add emphasis and drop several footnotes to his impressive execution of a tantalizing undertaking.[1]

In Cyprus, as in any international controversy, of course, international law and the international legal system were everywhere at all times: they provided the arena, they helped determine the participants, the weapons, and the rules, they shaped the action. The participants were sovereign states—a legal conception—and one entity that aspired to sovereign status, and the issues, indeed, went to the core of sovereignty. The weapons were those of diplomacy (and, unhappily, of force), among them the assertion and denial of legal rights and obligations. The rules included *pacta sunt servanda* (and claims of exception to the sanctity of treaties), the inviolability of sovereign territory, the law of the U.N. Charter against the use of force; some will add the principle of self-determination.

Professor Ehrlich tells how international law shaped and modified the view of governments as to their national interests, and their policies in pursuing those interests. To add a perspective, I abandon his chronological narrative for one with a different logic: one can examine the Cyprus case to see different uses of law in operation. Between crises, surely, Cyprus illustrates a principal purpose of law, to restrain and modify the behaviour of states. In part, perhaps, 'acculturation' and psychological inhibition keep officials from even considering gross violations of international obligation. In greater part, surely, by more-or-less conscious appraisal of cost and advantage, governments abide by their obligations because the fruits of violation do not seem worth the undesirable consequences. The law's restraining power is enhanced by the law's influence on the victim's response: a victim

* Hamilton Fish Professor of International Law and Diplomacy, Columbia University School of Law.

[1] I deal at length with the general subject in *How Nations Behave: Law and Foreign Policy* (1968).

will react, or react more vigorously, when he believes himself legally wronged, and, of course, the expectation of that response helps deter violation.

The restraining function of law inheres in international relations but, unhappily, it is difficult to observe and analyse. Usually one knows only that a possible action was not taken; at some times one can conclude that a government had the capacity, the interest, and the temptation to act; it is never possible to say how much law weighed among the forces that restrained action. The evidence is usually not available, and, at bottom, conclusive evidence can not exist, for if indeed one had access to all the records, if the actors told all, one could not be confident that one had reached the springs of official behaviour. And yet, those who have taken part in or studied the processes of government testify their certainty that law restrains in some degree in some ways. Often it deters forbidden action; when it does not wholly deter, it may yet delay, modify, or determine choices among alternatives.

When Great Britain became ready to abandon Cyprus, both Turkey and Greece had the interest to seize it and Turkey probably had also the capacity to do so. Both countries lacked a persuasive legal basis for claiming the Island, rendering it more likely that attempts by either to take it would be resisted. In addition, the law of the U.N. Charter and the near-certainty that one would have to answer for any violation in the U.N., increased the cost of unilateral seizure; it also put the use of force far lower in the scale of means which the governments were prepared to use to achieve their goals. The law against force, then, encouraged and allowed time and scope for diplomacy. The restraining, modifying influence of law can also be seen, in its different way, in Archbishop Makarios's hesitations, choices, and decisions in Professor Ehrlich's second 'case'.

The subtle, intricate workings of law are detectable also in the negotiations that led to the Zurich–London Accords. Turkey, no doubt, aware of the general limitations on the use of force, sought in the 1960 Agreements some release from those restraints, and even an affirmative legal support for the use of force if it became 'necessary'—hence Article IV of the Treaty of Guarantee. Whether an international lawyer would conclude that Article IV did or did not authorize the use of force, whether if so it is or is not valid in the face of the prohibitions of the U.N. Charter, the effect of the article was, at least, to render the governing law uncertain, weaken its deterrent effect, soften the objections and the responses of those affected by possible Turkish action, especially since they had agreed to that article. The 1960 Agreement, no doubt, also gave Turkish officials a sense of right to act, stronger than the sense of 'guilt' instilled by the U.N. Charter. It encouraged especially the kind of action (even if illegal) that is least likely to be deterred, the single act—a bombing attack—that presents a *fait accompli* and achieves a purpose that cannot be undone, as distinguished from continuing activities that permit opportunity for forces to gather to meet them.

Professor Ehrlich's first 'case', the British decision to relinquish sovereignty, shows law used differently, in the girding of legal strength to support policy. Of course, a government's perception of its rights will shape its policies, and Great Britain's view that it had sovereignty over Cyprus by virtue of the treaties of 1878 and 1923 contributed to and supported the policy of keeping it: with governments as with individuals, there is a tendency to wish to keep what one has, to believe it is right to do so, to avoid facing reasons why it might be desirable to agree to change. But those looking for lessons about law and its uses might ask also whether the British recognized that the strength in law of a treaty confirming a colonial relationship was being rapidly eroded by a new 'principle' of self-determination. Some will see this as a change in international law, with the Cyprus case bearing lessons about different rates of change in different laws in different political climates, about different governmental perceptions of change, and, obviously, different degrees of welcome or resistance to change.

Others will question whether 'self-determination' was or is a principle of international law. If so, the case has different lessons, for self-determination was surely an exploding political principle that attenuated the force of the law (the colonial treaty) as a weapon in international relations. Perhaps the victory of self-determination over colonial treaties should be seen as a special case of the effect on law of political international institutions, notably the United Nations. The United Nations, of course, is a 'legal' institution in that it was created by treaty (the U.N. Charter), the authority of its principal organs derive from that treaty, their purpose is in substantial part to carry out legal obligations in the treaty, and they often purport to be pursuing those treaty obligations. But in a different, deeper sense the U.N.

is a political not a legal institution and it deals with legal obligations in political ways. If, when the law and the relevant facts are
reasonably clear, the political choices in the U.N. are limited;
when they are not it has felt increasingly free to make political
determinations, propose or impose political results, rather than
render legal judgements.

For our purpose, it is clear, whatever a court might say about
the binding effect of colonial treaties, or about the legal quality
of a 'principle' of self-determination, the U.N. will lend its substantial influence to the destruction of Western colonial arrangements in Asia or Africa. Realistically, then, Great Britain could
not expect to stand on its legal case under the treaty. It might,
as a tactic, say it will never yield, but even for bargaining it is
difficult to stand on sands that have begun to shift. Compelled to
move, it effectively sought the support of law for a different
position—contained in the 1960 Agreement—with more attention
to realities in two relevant political arenas: the 1960 arrangements bound Greece and Turkey and substantially disarmed them
in both NATO and the U.N. But the 1960 solution created a
sovereign state of Cyprus, a legal entity with inevitable standing
and a voice in the United Nations, and one not effectively disarmed from challenging an arrangement that might be seen
as inconsistent with 'self-determination' or some related principle
paramount in the *zeitgeist* that pervades especially the United
Nations.

The 1960 Agreement is also an instance of legal imagination,
the use of ingenious legal machinery to escape dilemmas by novel
political effects. But what is ingenious does not always work,
particularly when ingenuity seeks to satisfy inconsistent 'principles' (self-determination for Cyprus but external 'veto' by
Turkey) and one of them is politically ascendant.

Professor Ehrlich's last case shows law in a lesser but still
interesting role: it provides a respectable way to accept defeat, to
make concessions, in particular to disarm domestic opposition.
In many countries, there are few circumstances in which the
explanation 'we were obligated to do it' does not silence most
opposition.

In all the cases, one sees law invoked to justify what has been
done. The cynic scoffs at such uses of law but his cynicism is
not wholly justified. That governments feel obliged to justify is
homage to virtue that also promotes it: because governments will

have to justify they are often impelled to do what is less difficult
to justify.

Of course, any generalizations from the Cyprus controversy
about the influence or non-influence of law in international relations must consider whether Cyprus is 'typical', and, if so, of
what. Disputes so serious that they invite the use of force and
threaten war imply immediate national interests that weigh heavily in a balance against the proximate costs of unlawfulness and
the longer-term national interests in law observance—in friendly
relations, in good repute, in stability, and order. Yet what nations
will fight for has, happily, changed. That Cyprus was primarily
a dispute between two states that were tied to each other in an
integrated alliance inevitably modified the forces that played in
the dispute, including the weight of law. Cyprus was further complicated by its rare blend of internal and international issues: the
establishment of a new state by an international covenant, with a
Constitution that, in major respects, could be amended only by
new international agreement, is a use of legal obligations and
legal mechanisms the effectiveness of which cannot be easily
generalized or judged by generalizations.

Students of law and politics move to a different arena when they
examine the influence of politics on law. All law, of course, is the
child of politics, of the policies which nations seek to further by
enacting them into law. Customary international law is the special
child of the mysterious process by which the actions and inactions,
the words and attitudes of nations, result in law. Both customary
and conventional law once made are altered during the course
and process of relations between nations. Cyprus, too, I have mentioned, has helped modify old law and perhaps made some new
law, but the process does not end, and cannot be arrested for
examination, and it is not always clear or agreed what law is
being made or how it will turn out. As Professor Ehrlich suggests,
some will see in the Archbishop's attempt to escape the 1960
Agreements a contribution to a doctrine that unequal treaties are
voidable. It is debatable whether Cyprus is in point for that
'doctrine': in context, Greece, Turkey, and the United Kingdom were not grossly unequal. The Government of Cyprus was
'less equal' but it was not strictly a party to the agreement but
rather its offspring. That it did not exist but very much wished
to, and succeeded (even if on conditions), does not suggest
'inequality' in a sense relevant to the proposed doctrine. The

Archbishop's claim to revision seems less well-based on in-equality of bargaining power than on some implication of 'self-determination' in that the Agreement sought to perpetuate a violation of the political independence of a sovereign country.

Professor Ehrlich seeks in Cyprus impetus for law or machinery that would provide for orderly revision of treaties. It is a commendable but difficult quest. Except where parties have anticipated and provided for revision, revision inevitably calls on *rebus sic stantibus* to give release from *pacta sunt servanda*. The release exists in principle but I am not hopeful about attempts to give it precise content or to create meaningful procedures applicable to all treaties. *Rebus* is the kind of doctrine that depends particularly on impartial development and application, as in domestic law by a judicial policy of non-enforcement. In international society release must generally depend on the parties themselves and if a state will sometimes release another or agree to revision it will not be likely to admit a legal compulsion to do so. In international relations a general obligation to 'bargain in good faith' about treaty revision does not promise more than the existing Charter obligation to settle all international disputes by peaceful means. Cyprus may indeed show that, as regards those obligations that run afoul of some 'superior' principle or mood, revision will come and bargaining about revision, surely, cannot long be resisted.

COMMENT

Edwin C. Hoyt *

In thinking about the ways in which international law affects national decision-making, it may be helpful to have in mind an analytical framework.[1] I should like first to outline such a framework and then to discuss the Cyprus case in that context.

The continuing process of action and reaction in international relations may be diagrammed (assuming only two states are involved) as follows:

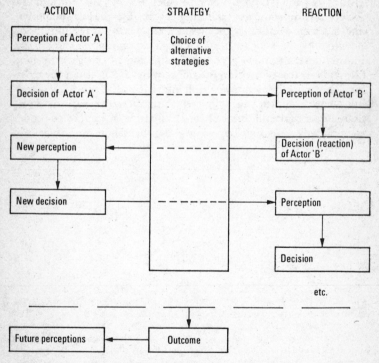

* Professor of Political Science, University of New Mexico.

[1] The framework is, of course, tentative and may need revision as thinking is improved by suggestive insights from new cases.

While 'the real world' may determine how things finally come out, it does not determine national decisions. In the words of Kenneth Boulding, 'The people whose decisions determine the policies and actions of nations do not respond to the "objective" facts of the situation, whatever that may mean, but to their "image" of the situation'.[2] This means that the analysis of national decision-making is concerned with perceptions. What is important for our investigation is not what the law is (always a debatable question), but how it is perceived by the decision-makers.

Here it may be useful to look first at decision-making in the nation which initiates a demand for change (Actor A in the diagram). Without hoping to provide an exhaustive list, it is easy to think of some elements in the perception of the situation which are likely to be present. One would be a perception of need for change, of dissatisfaction with the existing situation. A second element may be an appreciation of the legal situation, including relevant treaties, customary rules and the vested rights of other parties. This element may not enter into the perception if it has not come to the attention of the decision-makers (the role of legal advisers here comes to mind), but it is likely to be present and to be considered in relation to anticipated reactions of the opposite party. A third significant element may be a factor of 'responsiveness'— the degree of hostility or friendliness perceived in the nation's relationship with the opposite party and consequent predisposition, or the lack of it, to respond to the needs of the other party.[3]

---

[2] Boulding, 'National Images and International Systems', 3 J. Conflict Resolution 120 (1959); cf. Harold and Margaret Sprout, *Foundations of International Politics* (D. Van Nostrand Company, Inc., New York, 1962), pp. 49, 124 ff. The relationship of perceptions to decisions is further elaborated in Joseph de Rivera, *The Psychological Dimensions of Foreign Policy* (Charles E. Merrill Publishing Company, Columbus, 1968).

[3] Deutsch first pointed to this factor as an essential background condition for international integration. Karl W. Deutsch *et al.*, *Political Community and the North Atlantic Area* (Princton University Press, 1957). Pruitt's research concerning an office of the Department of State dealing with a group of 'friendly' nations indicated that 'responsiveness affects the choice tactics during controversies. The more responsive a person feels toward another nation, the more likely is he to want his nation to use *mild tactics* in dealing with the other nation . . .' Dean G. Pruitt, 'Definition of the Situation as a Determinant of International Action', in *International Behavior*, ed. Herbert C. Kelman (Holt, Rinehart & Winston, New York, 1965), pp. 393–432, 398. 'Mild tactics' would presumably include discussions of legality.

A fourth element is perception of the nations' political capabilities with respect to the desired change (which may in turn be affected by whether the demands to be made will be perceived by outsiders as legitimate), and a fifth relevant element may be a perception of military capabilities in event of hostilities.

For the decision-makers of Actor B, the first element in their perception of the situation is the action of A to which they must react. Next in importance may be their perception of their legal rights. Third may be a perception of the practical consequences of acceptance of A's demand. Also present, as in the case of Actor A, are perceptions of 'responsiveness', political capabilities and military capabilities.

Both A and B, beyond the need to act or react, may perceive a choice of alternative action strategies. Perceptions of international law may affect this choice in ways that have been noted by Fisher. It may be perceived that one course of conduct will appear to others more legitimate than another, and should therefore provoke less opposition from the opposite party or win third-party support. There may also be perceptions of long-term effects of the precedents that will be set, either as they may affect other substantive interests of the actor or as they may affect the future of the international legal system and its institutions. Securing formalization of the desired change in treaty form may increase the stability of the desired outcome. And finally, international law may influence the outcome in bargaining situations if an obvious perception of legal right makes more credible a threat to use force, or if legal doctrines suggest salient points at which compromise can be reached.[4]

We may well find that there are significant differences among types of nations or types of decision-makers in respect to the legal element in perceptions of situations. Nations newly independent after a successful revolt against colonial legality may retain for some time a revolutionary point of view toward the international legal order, despite the socializing effects of admission to membership in the international system. Nations which see themselves as having major responsibility for world order may be more concerned about the general impact of new precedents than are

[4] Compare Schelling's discussion of the importance of conspicuousness, or saliency, in determining meeting points in 'games of coordination'. Thomas C. Schelling, *The Strategy of Conflict* (Oxford University Press, New York, 1963), pp. 53-91.

nations which confront international law as a system largely set by others. Concern for the effects of precedent on other immediate or specific interests of the acting nation may be a more universal consideration. The examination of different types of cases should help us to develop hypotheses as to such differences among nations.

Since decision-makers respond to their perception of the situation rather than to 'the objective facts' or 'reality', we do not need to consider whether their legal analysis is sound or unsound in order to calculate the role of law in decision-making. We should distinguish analytically between the perceptions that affect their decisions and the arguments they make later in self-justification, though we may note that their perception of the situation may include an appreciation that a colourable, even if dubious, legal argument can be made in defence of a certain course of action.[5]

The evidence concerning decisions by the four governments most immediately concerned in the Cyprus problem remains, unfortunately, very speculative. It indicates, for one thing, how much more difficult it is for Americans to obtain information concerning decision-making by foreign governments than it is for them to obtain information concerning their own government's decisions. Very much more detailed information is available to us, clearly, about American decision-making in regard to Greek–Turkish Aid, the Berlin Blockade, Korea, Suez, the Dominican Republic, or Vietnam. Yet despite this handicap, it is possible, as Mr. Ehrlich has done, to make educated guesses as to what went on.

[5] An example which well illustrates this last point is the American decision of June 1950 to intervene between the Chinese Communists and the island of Formosa (Taiwan). Five months before that decision was taken, it had been suggested by some that there was a legal basis for intervention because, while Formosa had been delivered to Chinese possession in 1945, it had not been finally separated from Japan so long as no peace treaty had been signed. The possibility of acting on that theory had been considered and rejected in January 1950, and Secretary Acheson then characterized it as a legal 'quibble'. But in August 1950 the previously rejected argument became the defence used in the Security Council against the Peking Government's complaint that the American protection of Formosa constituted aggression against China. Based on these facts, I concluded that 'law was not a factor in the Formosa decision'. Hoyt, 'The United States Reaction to the Korean Attack', 55 Am. J. Int'l. L., 58–66 (1961). I now realize that I was wrong. While the decision to change course in view of the Korean War was primarily a political decision, it would have been very much less likely had it not been for the decision-makers' perception of a colourable legal basis in the previously rejected theory.

To me, it seems most likely that the British decision to relinquish sovereignty in 1958 was taken despite the perception that they had a clear legal right to retain the Island, based not only on long possession, but also on the Treaty of Lausanne to which both Greece and Turkey were parties. Perhaps it can be argued that Britain should have viewed self-determination as a legal norm, but they did not so perceive it. So far as it affected their decisions, then, law was a consideration justifying continued British occupation of the Island. But by 1957 other perceived elements of the situation were negative. The attractiveness of British police actions in the Middle East, for which Cyprus was the staging area, was diminished by the Suez experience, and perceptions of the political and military costs of resisting the Cypriots' demand now outweighed the perception of legal rectitude.

What was Archbishop Makarios's perception of the situation in 1963, when he decided to demand revision of the Cypriot Constitution? First of all, there was evidently a strong perception of a need for change—the Constitution of 1960 was no longer acceptable to Makarios. As to the perceived legal situation, it was clear—a written constitution, unamendable (at least without consent of all interested parties), and supported by the Treaty of Guarantee.[6] International law must therefore have been perceived as an obstacle to be overcome. The character of Makarios's régime helps to explain his behaviour. His viewpoint was not that of the government of a well-established state. He was accustomed to the role of a rebel against constituted authority, seeking by political means to overturn an intolerable legal state of affairs. Relations with the Turks were characterized by a lack of responsiveness. Makarios must have perceived that Turkey, and to a lesser extent Britain, would resist his demand for change and that this resistance would be strengthened by those powers' perception of having the law on their side. But counteracting this disadvantage were Makarios's perceptions of his own political and military capabilities, the advantage of locally preponderant power, and the possibility of mobilizing outside support from the Soviet Union and the anti-

---

[6] This arrangement placed limits on Cyprus's sovereignty in the interest of international peace, in effect making Cyprus, outside the British bases, a neutralized area. Compare the limitations imposed on Austria by the State Treaty for the Re-establishment of an Independent and Democratic Austria, 15 May 1955, T.I.A.S. 3298, 217 U.N.T.S. 223.

colonial bloc. As Ehrlich points out, the choice of strategies favoured a request for revision and an appeal to the General Assembly. But the fact that a legal argument was later made in the U.N., to the effect that the 1960 treaties were unequal and therefore void, does not mean that legal considerations significantly influenced Makarios's decision. The demand for revision coupled with going to the U.N. was probably preferred over outright denunciation of the treaties because to adopt the more 'reasonable' course gave a better chance of mobilizing political support and of at least delaying Turkish military action.

Makarios proceeded meanwhile with his programme of unilateral revision, and Turkish and British decision-makers were forced to consider how they should react to Makarios's actions. In the chain of action and reaction, part of Turkey's response to Makarios became the demands made on Greece in November 1967. This put Greece in the position of having to decide how to respond, as Turkey and Britain had had to do earlier.

What part did international law play in the perceptions of the Turkish and British Governments?[7] They of course perceived Makarios's intent to modify the 1960 settlement. They undoubtedly were strongly conscious of their own legal rights. They almost certainly perceived that their rights would atrophy if they did not exercise them, and they must have perceived that other states would expect them to do something in support of those rights. There was more than colourable justification even for the use of force (Article IV of the treaty). At least they might expect that this element of legitimacy would substantially weaken or neutralize possible action against them in the United Nations. This is the kind of situation in which the existence of vested legal rights becomes itself an impetus to action. This legal element in their perceptions may have tipped the balance for Turkey in favour of intervention. The outcome of British deliberations was different—a difference which is accounted for by the other elements of the perception, most notably the political importance of the issue, which was much less in Britain's case than in Turkey's, where domestic opinion was strongly activated. In both cases political capabilities were perceived as limited, but there was a perceived capability for military intervention. For Britain, the perceived long-term costs of intervention were too high. For

[7] The Turkish community on Cyprus clearly relied on strong law (the 1960 Accords) to offset military weakness.

Turkey, weighed against their stronger interests, the costs of intervention were perceived as marginally acceptable.

The Turks nevertheless confined their direct military measures against Makarios to what were essentially warning actions. A perceived danger of escalation was probably one reason for caution. Another may have been quasi-legal—recognition of a consensus that defensive use of force should be kept to minimum proportions and be of a character which would not foreclose opportunities for the United Nations to act to end the fighting. But the threat of stronger action was made credible by its legal basis— Article IV of the treaty, and in both instances it produced results (the sending of the U.N. force after the first 'warning flight', the ceasefire after the August air action).[8]

The Turks ultimately decided to demand withdrawal of Greek troops from Cyprus. Their perception of the legal situation probably entered strongly into the choice of this strategy. Greece was in clear violation of the 1960 treaty by its commitment of troops in Cyprus far beyond the numbers allowed in the treaty and the treaty also specified Turkey's legal interest. A precedent supporting such a demand, in a much weaker legal case, had been set by the United States in the Cuban missile crisis. The Turks perceived a need to act if they were to prevent further erosion of Turkish legal rights. Greece's interest in Cyprus was perceived as less than Makarios's, indicating better political prospects that the Greeks would comply with Turkey's demands than that Makarios would. The demands on Greece would seem more legitimate to members of the General Assembly than would an immediate move to escalate the conflict in Cyprus. The demands on Greece carried the implied threat, however, of Turkish military action if Greece did not comply, a threat again made credible by the legitimacy of the Turkish case.

Just as action by the U.N. to send a U.N. Force to Cyprus in March of 1964 had been a means of relieving Turkey of political pressure to take further forcible measures at that time, and a legally correct compromise that Makarios could accept, so now the formula of an appeal by the U.N. Secretary-General, backed by the Security Council, for phased withdrawal of all non-Cypriot forces, and for all parties to refrain from military intervention in Cyprus, provided a legal interim settlement which

[8] The Cypriot Government's argument that Article IV did not justify the use of force did not affect their perception that the Turks thought it did.

satisfied Turkey's essential demand in a way that Greece could accept. Law here filled its function of providing a dignified path for retreat from positions that have become too dangerous or costly. These are also illustrations of the way legal formulas offer salient compromise solutions.

None of the principal parties in the Cyprus case appears to have been motivated to any significant degree by concern for improving the international system.

COMMENT

*Hans A. Linde**

i

IN reading Professor Ehrlich's well-informed and thoughtful review of four national decisions concerning Cyprus, it is important to keep in mind the purpose of his study and others that are to follow. The task that these studies have set themselves is to trace and evaluate the uses of legal premises and legal arguments in the shaping of the national decisions being studied. As the author puts it:

> The primary focus of this analysis is the role of legal norms and institutions in each government's decision-making process. Within that framework, the study is particularly concerned with how law was brought to bear by foreign governments and international institutions on national decision-makers.

He goes on to pose this question more specifically: how international law delimits national goals and means, to what extent the international appeal of adversary claims depends on the adversaries' legal positions, whether legal procedures and institutions may mobilize external economic or military (i.e. 'real') pressure on national decisions, and how effective legal procedures and institutions are in containing and resolving conflicts.

Posed in this way, the questions describe an empirical inquiry. This corresponds to the objective described in the Foreword by Professor Roger Fisher. It is clear, Professor Fisher writes, that responsible actors in international affairs talk and behave in ways that reflect 'international law' in a variety of roles. The object is to identify and examine these roles of law in actual operation in order, not to measure law quantitatively against other factors of decision, but to gain insights for making law work better. We start, then, with a thoroughly instrumentalist perspective which is eager to move beyond classical debates about methodology and 'jurisprudential and philosophical questions' in order to learn from the stuff of history itself. Such empiricism is both congenial and needed. But I believe it is essential to recognize

* Professor of Law, University of Oregon School of Law.

that the inquiry remains analytical as well as empirical. To determine what role law played *in fact*, and how, presupposes that we recognize evidence of law when we see it. It presupposes either stipulated or implicit criteria for 'law'. When these criteria are not in doubt, an inquiry may well ask the wholly empirical question: 'To what extent did international law *affect* governmental decisions concerning Cyprus?' And we may, with Professor Ehrlich, find that the answer is 'Quite a bit'. But I fear we cannot escape also asking the analytical question, 'To what extent do the phenomena shown here to affect governmental decisions constitute international *law*?' This theoretical component of the inquiry is as indispensable as the empirical, if the inferences of a case study are not to resemble those that might be drawn by a priest and a psychiatrist examining the efficacy of prayer in a patient's recovery.

Professor Ehrlich takes pains not to overstate his empirical case—how much difference the legal considerations and arguments actually made to the decisions he describes—and he warns us that a focus singling out any one among many factors necessarily tends to exaggerate that factor's significance. Moreover, he must often speculate that one party 'may have' anticipated legal arguments that might be made by another, and that certain considerations 'must have' been taken into account. This uncertainty about the precise impact of law on behaviour seems to me inescapable, and I do not think it detracts materially from the value of these studies. Even in domestic law it cannot be easy to determine whether and how law finally shaped a decision, unless the law plainly pointed to one decision while other factors pulled toward a different one. Our present concern with Professor Ehrlich's studies is not with what they tell us of the diplomatic history of Cyprus, but with what they tell us about international law. For this purpose, Ehrlich's reconstruction of known facts and hypotheses is perfectly adequate even if some of his guesses should prove to be historically wrong.

What can empirical studies like these tell us about international law? What useful hypotheses can be tested or suggested by the evidence?

It is not too difficult to compile an inventory of 'roles' of international law or 'ways' in which it enters into national decisions. Many of them are illustrated in Ehrlich's Cyprus studies, and for those that are not, other illustrations can readily be found. Some of them go to the substance of national policy, some to procedure, some to form.

The latter roles of law are easiest to show. International law offers a formal framework for pursuing national foreign policy. If and when England, Greece, and Turkey could settle their mutual interests in Cyprus, the form of a treaty was available to embody that settlement. The diplomatic procedures for asserting these interests, for determining whether a basis for negotiation existed, and for negotiating a treaty were well known. The system provides a recognized form and channel of communication. Among those three governments, none had to ask 'whom can we talk to about this' and 'how'. If that seems a slight achievement of a legal system, the recent history preceding the Paris negotiations about Vietnam reminds us otherwise.

Even more obvious is the role of legal forms and legal procedures when national policy is brought into the forum of an international organization. Ehrlich shows how the law of the organization inescapably frames the terms of debate over the forum's jurisdiction, over its internal procedures, over its potential for action—quite apart from whether the law also determines the substance of the organization's decisions. Governments must be prepared to fight those jurisdictional and procedural battles in legal terms or accept whatever costs attach to non-participation.

Law is shown also to enter into the substance of policy beyond these formal and procedural functions, and not only in the sense that the available international procedures and institutions affect what kind of steps are open to governments. Governments, and not only democratic ones, usually need to *state* a policy in order to be able to carry it out as a policy. They have a need to explain the policy, and to explain becomes to *justify*; policy tends to be explained in the rhetoric of claims of right and wrong. Claims of right and disclaimers of wrong enter into the policy-making processes deep within the national societies themselves—between hawks and doves, say, or between civilian and military cabinet members, between representatives of economic or ethnic interests, between the government and its opposition. The choice of rhetoric is often shaped by the rhetoric of claims under international law: self-defence, neutrality, aggression, self-determination, non-intervention, sovereignty, protection of nationals, standing by one's commitments, etc. Moreover, the choice of a theory in international law often has far-reaching consequences under domestic law, especially when the question involves 'war' or something less, as in U.S. actions in Korea and in Indo-China. So it is suggested that the language of law shapes a nation's and its rulers' perception of what is a thinkable object of policy, antecedent to any calculation of the possible external responses and consequences of unlawful action—that law forestalls embryonic national delinquencies not by abortion but by contraception. The same built-in constraint may keep some technically possible *means* of policy from even getting on a decision-making agenda.

Useful as it is to identify such a list of the uses of 'law' in policy and to work it out in greater detail, the behavioural approach must guard against proving either too little or too much. To show that the language of policy since time immemorial has been a language of claims of right tells us something about language, but how much does it tell us about law? If we observe that military commanders throughout history, whenever they have preferred to seek a voluntary surrender rather than a battle, have found it necessary to identify responsible leaders among the opponents and to communicate with them, through properly authenticated messengers, interpreters, etc., about comprehensible terms of occupation, tribute, hostages, ransom, or future alliance, we may learn something about the essential strategies of organized adversary confrontations. But to isolate the element of 'law' in these phenomena it seems necessary to go beyond such empirical observations of rhetoric and of forms of interaction. As undifferentiated evidence of 'law' in international affairs, these observations claim too much, but to fail to discriminate among them may claim too little. It seems necessary to distinguish between an observation that a policy makes use of 'legal' forms and 'legal' rhetoric as *instruments* (conceding that policy is sometimes influenced by the very choice among these and their alternatives) and an observation that a policy is deflected by recognition of a legal *obligation*. It seems necessary to ask whether we identify 'international law' in the same sense when we observe references to British sovereignty over Cyprus in the House of Commons, when we see the Security Council tied up for hours over the order of speakers under its Provisional Rule 27, when Cypriot leaders invoke the right of 'self-determination', or when private counsel are asked to advise clients about the status of legal transactions after unilateral changes in the Cyprus constitution, in the light of the Zurich–London Accords of 1960.

ii

What gives the Cyprus studies their special interest is that they involve the interrelationship of overlapping legal orders. The question of 'decolonization' of Cyprus could, and probably would, have arisen under traditional international law as it stood before World War I, if the League of Nations, the Kellogg–Briand pact, the United Nations, and NATO had never been thought of. In the 1960 Accords the interested parties used the instruments of this traditional legal order to create a mutually acceptable regime for their interests. But by then the United Kingdom, Greece, and Turkey were members also of the North Atlantic Treaty Organization and of the United Nations. And in the latter organization, many of their fellow members were former colonies whose views of legality reflected a greater sense of affinity with the position of Cyprus than with the three other parties to that régime. The existence of these international organizations, with their distinct functions and with the objectives each government would pursue within them, certainly complicated the political task of formulating a policy for Cyprus. The question for analysis is whether among these political consequences of the post-war institutions it is possible to separate any distinctly legal constraints on policy.

When the United Kingdom, Greece, and Turkey signed the United Nations Charter, did they legally commit themselves not to use such devices of international law as the 1960 Treaty of Guarantee? Or to use them only subject to overriding action by the Security Council? Or also subject to 'recommendations' by the General Assembly? Suppose Greece could have been persuaded to apply to Cyprus the NATO procedures for settling disputes within that organization. Could a non-NATO member of the United Nations have made a persuasive case that, for instance, the use of a NATO instead of a United Nations Force on the Island was not only outrageous, aggressive, neo-colonialist, etc., but also unlawful?

These questions would concern especially England, which throughout the events recounted by Professor Ehrlich occupied the key position as the power relinquishing sovereignty, as a guarantor of the 1960 Accords, the leading European member of NATO, and as a permanent member of the United Nations with the power of veto. They would concern also the United States, as one factor in its calculation of how much effort to invest in keeping the crisis in the eastern Mediterranean 'in the family' and out of the reach of Soviet political participation and Soviet vetoes. They are questions of the scope the Charter leaves nations for legal régimes to accommodate and safeguard their mutual interests at a less than universal level, and particularly for regional arrangements.

Regional arrangements are the specific object of Chapter VIII of the Charter. Ehrlich recounts how Cyprus demanded in the Security Council a clear answer whether the Guarantor Powers under the 1960 Treaty claimed any right of military intervention, how Turkey later concluded that it would find no sympathy in the United Nations for such a claim to support its bombing raid and fell back on 'self-defence', and how the British Government evaded a squarely affirmative answer both in the Security Council and in the House of Commons. These are perfectly understandable diplomatic positions. Precisely because they are understandable positions, given the exigencies of the respective forums, they are only modest evidence for a legal analysis of regional or other special associations. The questions appear here in the post-Suez setting in which England in fact was not eager to resume responsibility in Cyprus as a guarantor, nor did it and the United States in fact choose to force the issue of the primary jurisdiction of NATO or the United Nations. But suppose the political facts had been otherwise. Suppose a strong United Kingdom, supported by the United States, wished to assert the prerogative of the Treaty of Guarantee or internal NATO processes and to back them up with Security Council vetoes if needed. Could a respectable legal argument be made for the legitimacy of such a course, or would it be so weak as to inhibit that choice of policy?

Upon examination of possible objections, both the 1960 Accords and NATO appear to meet reasonable criteria of 'regional arrangements' by geography and by whatever rudiments of organization and procedures beyond a mere treaty of alliance the concept may require. And nothing in the Charter's provisions for regional arrangements suggests that they must be directed against external threats rather than at disputes internal to the region. To the contrary, Article 52 of the Charter obligates members to seek 'pacific settlement of local disputes through such regional arrangements or by such regional agencies before referring them to the Security Council'. The question is what limits Article 53 places upon further internal action under the provisions of a regional organization or 'arrangement'.

The pertinent clauses of Article 53 read:

1. The Security Council shall, where appropriate, utilize such regional arrangements or agencies for enforcement action under its authority. But no enforcement action shall be taken under regional arrangements or by regional agencies without the authorization of the Security Council [with the exception of measures against enemy states of World War II].

The double reference to 'enforcement action' creates a puzzle of Charter interpretation: what kind of action is 'enforcement' action, and what is being 'enforced'?

These terms are not defined elsewhere in the Charter. However, it seems clear that they refer to action described as the use of force, or of armed force, when taken by the Security Council under Chapter VII of the Charter, particularly Articles 42 *et seq.* The International Court of Justice so stated in the United Nations Expenses Case, in which it also held that the United Nations Forces in Egypt and in the Congo did not represent enforcement action. Possibly the term might extend also to the non-military but coercive sanctions described in Article 41. What such action by the Security Council 'enforces' is not necessarily an obligation, under the Charter or otherwise, that has been violated by anyone; it may enforce a measure voted by the Security Council itself with the sole objective of maintaining or restoring international peace and security.

For this purpose, the Council 'shall' utilize regional arrangements or agencies 'where appropriate'. This sentence of Article 53 alone would offer a regional big power—like our hypothetical British Government bent on maintaining the initiative in Cyprus —a legal ground for argument that the 1960 Accords were precisely the appropriate arrangement in that region even for action under the authority of the Security Council, an argument backed by a defensible veto if other members pursued different Council action in disregard of the regional arrangement.

More important, however—since a Security Council vote to utilize a regional arrangement for enforcement action can hardly be expected—is what 'enforcement action' the regional arrangement may or may not take without Council authorization. Could action be taken within the terms of Article IV of the Treaty of Guarantee 'with the sole aim of re-establishing the state of affairs' in Cyprus? As far as the nature of the action taken is concerned, the double use of the phrase in Article 53 implies that such regional acts are 'enforcement action' as would derive from Chapter VII if taken by the Security Council. Consequently Article 53 would not require Security Council authorization, under the view of UNEF and ONUC taken in the United Nations Expenses Case, for placing forces under the Treaty of Guarantee or NATO in Cyprus by consent of the parties. Can binding consent be given in advance? Does action by a regional agency upon such prior consent become 'enforcement action' requiring Security Council authorization—though it does not purport to 'enforce' the Charter or a Council resolution—if the consent is withdrawn at the time of action? Or must the regional action, to come within the restraints of Article 53, be a use of force which but for Security Council approval would violate Article 2(4)?

In short, the question of Article 53 is whether groups of nations may develop for themselves effective regional institutions for maintaining security within the region itself. It is not too much to say that the tension between the regional and the universalist approaches displayed in Article 53 has for more than twenty years been the main issue in competing conceptions of the future development of international order. There is no reason to expect that this issue will be soon resolved in favour of universalism. Nor is the pull toward regional arrangements always a cover for superpower hegemony, as in the case of United States actions in the Caribbean, or of the 'Brezhnev doctrine' among the members of the Warsaw Pact.[1] If Western Europe, for instance, eventually moves beyond a common market toward sharing functions creating an even greater mutual dependency, particularly functions essential to defence, it will need some capacity to respond to an internal crisis that might threaten a vital link in the regional system. In the case of Cyprus, similarly, the priority of regional over United Nations jurisdiction might have been pressed more forcefully if the exclusion of external participation there had been

---

[1] The conflict between regionalism and national sovereignty in a universal system has recently been sharply stated, with a bitter attack on claims of regionism for their systemic implications, in Franck and Weisband, 'The Johnson–Brezhnev Doctrines: Verbal Behavior Analysis of Superpower Confrontations', in Policy Papers of the New York University Center for International Studies, vol. 3, no. 2 (1970).

deemed as vital to NATO as, for instance, the Dominican Republic was considered to the American regional system.

Where the constitutional reality of the international system has moved toward regional primacy, the arguments about the constitutional law of the system have shown the strain. Past United Nations debates have characteristically reflected the shifting tactical needs of the parties with respect to the legitimacy of regional action. The defenders of such actions generally find themselves forced in the direction of a claim of 'self-defence' under Article 51 as the only all-purpose escape-hatch from the apparent Security Council monopoly on the use of force. Ehrlich illustrates this by the legal dilemma confronting Turkey in 1964 despite its position under the Treaty of Guarantee. For the United States, the State Department's Legal Adviser has sought another way to legitimize Inter-American regional actions under Article 53 without the Article 51 prerequisite of an 'armed attack'. This was to suggest that (1) the Security Council 'authorization' mentioned in Article 53 can be provided after the regional action is taken; (2) it need be no more than a preambular 'taking note' of that action; and (3) it might even be satisfied by inaction by the Council. '[Surely] it is not more surprising to say that failure of the Security Council to disapprove regional action amounts to authorization within the meaning of Article 53', he wrote later, 'than it was to say that the abstention and even the absence of a permanent member of the Security Council met the requirement of Article 27(3) for "the concurring votes of the permanent members . . ."'[2]

With all respect to a once and now again colleague, it seems a good deal more surprising. Whatever one may think of the fortuitous precedent of the Security Council's Korean action in the absence of the Soviet delegation, that Charter interpretation left the choice and the responsibility to permit or to block Security Council action with the permanent members of the Council. By contrast, the proposed escape from Article 53 simply stands the article on its head, as if it read: enforcement action may be taken under regional arrangements or by regional agencies unless the Security Council forbids it. This reversal of action and response is rather more reminiscent of President Truman's argument that he could constitutionally seize the steel industry since he at once asked

[2] Chayes, 'Law and the Quarantine of Cuba', 41 Foreign Affairs 550, 556 (1963).

Congress to endorse or over-rule his action—an argument rejected by the U.S. Supreme Court. And affirmative disapproval by the Security Council, unlike Congress, is of course likely to be impossible, nor could it undo the unauthorized action already taken.

To save a legal capacity for internal regional action, as distinguished from individual or collective self-defence against armed attack under Article 51, was and is a worthwhile objective. But there is a better theory for this than one which would ascribe to the Security Council a fictitious 'authorization' which the Council did not and would not give, a theory which does less violence to the Charter text and to its underlying political assumptions about the functions of regional organizations. This theory would recognize that action which might fit Article 53's term 'enforcement action under regional arrangements or by regional agencies' may be internal to the regional arrangement, or it may be directed against a non-member. When directed at a non-member of the arrangement, or when it purports to 'enforce' the Charter or a Security Council resolution, the regional action requires Council authorization, unless it satisfies Article 51. But action is not 'enforcement action' unless without such authorization it would violate Article 2(4)—i.e. threaten or use force 'against the territorial integrity or political independence of any state, or in any other manner inconsistent with the Purposes of the United Nations'. And nations can agree to provide among themselves procedures and institutional mechanisms that would be unlawful, under Article 2(4) or otherwise, in the absence of such agreement —call it consent, or waiver, or even a tiny step toward regional confederation. For the duration of a nation's adherence to such an arrangement, then, much internal regional action under it would not be a violation of territorial integrity, or of political independence, or of Article 1, section 1, unless it went beyond the scope of the intra-regional consent, or unless the affected party could plausibly claim that its consent had never been freely given, or unless the Security Council affirmatively asserted a superior responsibility under its own Charter authority—the hierarchical situation Professor Ehrlich finds in the presence of United Nations forces in Cyprus at the time of the Turkish bombings in 1964.

iii

From this conventional legal theorizing about the 'right' answer to a question of international law, let us revert to how the law affects international practice.

Professor Ehrlich shows us much 'law' in the form of arguments which were made in support of national action or national claims, other arguments which may have been considered and found wanting, and potential counter-arguments which may have been anticipated and taken into account in shaping national positions. Earlier in these comments I suggested that the mere phrasing of policy in the language of claims of right is not in itself evidence of law in action. Are some of the roles of legal terminology more 'law' than others? I think that we in fact do recognize such a spectrum of roles or functions, within which some are more 'law' than others. This recognition should help both in the task of scholarly analysis and in answering Ehrlich's 'most important' question: what steps can be taken to strengthen the contribution of law.

The striking fact about the display of legal arguments in these Cyprus studies is how 'arguments' as a decisional factor take on importance in direct proportion to the importance of the forum. The review of legal arguments in the Cyprus setting adds up, in fact, to a study in the law of international organizations. It is not the existence and weight of the legal arguments as such, but the constellation of political factors leading to the use of the United Nations forum that enhanced the importance of the legal components in the various decisions concerning Cyprus.

Once an issue is brought to debate in an institutional forum, by one's own choice or that of others, each participant's arguments become inescapably 'legal' in the sense that they are shaped by the terms that define the jurisdiction, the procedures, and the substantive objectives of the institutional forum. They must reflect also an estimate of how far the support of other participants will depend on offering them a compelling or at least a tenable legal premiss for the desired political decision. The costly alternative to this attention to the law of the forum is not to participate at all. The cost may be prohibitive in relation to national considerations of domestic and foreign interests that are not measured simply by the nation's relative 'power'. England, for instance, would not pay the price of choosing that alternative against investigation of Greek charges by the European Commission on Human Rights in 1956, as Greece in turn chose to do in 1969.

When we focus on the role of international law in national decisions, these observations state only the commonplace, that careful attention to legal claims takes on importance to the extent that the actors place a value on third-party judgement or on maintaining the effectiveness of a legal institution. What do the same observations mean when the focus is not on the role of law in behaviour, but on the analysis of 'law'? The Cyprus studies illustrate, particularly when compared with other contemporary conflicts involving force, how various premises of similar legal formality properly belong at different ends of the spectrum of phenomena described as 'law'.

Thus at one end of the spectrum we have the treaty obligations assumed directly by the parties to the United Nations Charter, without any action by the organization, specifically in Article 2, sections 2, 3, 4, and in Chapter XI with respect to non-self-governing territories. At the other end of the spectrum we have the provisions of Chapters IV–VII and XV which define the procedures by which the organization could assign to its Secretary-General the mission and the means of stationing a United Nations force in Cyprus. Formally, these treaty provisions qualify identically as international law. Functionally, they have little in common.

The obligations of Article 2, sections 2, 3, and 4 (reinforced by Article 33) assert a general good faith commitment to settle international disputes peacefully and to refrain from the threat or use of force in international relations. Divorced from the organizational premises of the Charter, they might be found in a general non-aggression treaty. What role such commitments play·in national decisions and in international political rhetoric is entirely predictable on the record of the Kellogg–Briand pact, of numerous bilateral non-aggression treaties, and of the Charter itself in the contemporary conflicts that have not been brought before the United Nations or another forum. To the extent that they enter into internal or external debate over national action, such provisions invariably pose the same juxtaposition of the commitment to avoid force and its counterpart or exception: pursuit of a national security interest that is characterized as 'defensive', as a legitimate response to the actions of another. This is not to say that the commitment is meaningless or useless.

At a minimum, it accepts the premiss that the pursuit of a national interest by force calls for some justification. But it is doubtful whether our analysis of the role of law gains more than it loses by describing this mere formal commitment to peace, with its countervailing exception, as 'law'—at least in so far as it bears upon the decision of the primary actors, as distinguished from the decisions of third parties.

The function of the institutional provisions of the Charter and of resolutions adopted under them is quite different. From the standpoint of the United Nations Force in Cyprus, and of all the many parties in and out of Cyprus which in various ways were concerned with the force, these documents are the guts of international law. They are at the opposite extreme on the spectrum of 'law'. In a decision of England, Greece, or Turkey on the use of its forces in Cyprus, only one element of policy would be the web of relevant commitments and expectations, whether these be 'legal' or not. By contrast, without the international law of the Charter and United Nations resolutions, UNFICYP would not exist at all. Unlike the separate parties' instruments of national policy, however much- or little-constrained they are by national calculation of various normative relationships, UNFICYP— the instrument actually deployed to keep peace in Cyprus— is wholly a creature of international law. Without it, Swedish and Irish soldiers would not have the slightest business guarding Othello's tower.

Experience with the United Nations Forces in the Middle East, established under Secretary-General Dag Hammerskjöld in 1956 and withdrawn by Secretary-General U Thant in 1967, and in the Congo has demonstrated this totally different role of international law—the operational importance of the terms of authorizations, of instructions, of agreements on furnishing troops, on financing, on lines of command, on host country consent, on status of forces, etc. The constant relevance of legal premisses to international instrumentalities is shown not only by the evolution of the controversies that finally led to the United Nations Expenses Case in the International Court of Justice and the crisis over financing, but also by the unhappy history of the 'Good Faith Accord' by which Hammarskjöld had hoped to constrain abrupt Egyptian withdrawal of its consent to UNEF.[3] This

---

[3] See Garvey, 'United Nations Peacekeeping and Host State Consent', 64 Am. J. Int'l L. 241 (1970), and more generally, Nathanson, 'Constitutional

essential importance of law to international instrumentalities is true of less universal institutions than the United Nations, though perhaps softened in the setting of co-operation in a joint rather than an adversary enterprise. I do not mean, of course, that secretaries-general or other international agencies respond to legal considerations to the exclusion of political ones. They are, however, dependent on legal justifications for all their actions in a way in which national governments are not; and so, therefore, are national governments in dealing with them.

In studying how international law affects national decisions, then, we are not observing 'law' in the same sense when, for instance, Archbishop Makarios considers invoking 'sovereign equality' or *rebus sic stantibus* to justify escape from the 1960 Accords as we would if he were to ask that a United Nations UNFICYP company move its base half a mile to a different location. But between 'general principles' at one end and the operating manuals of international agencies at the other, where on the spectrum may evidence of law in action be found, if we are not to take as evidence of law every phenomenon that can be observed in the forms or language of law? This, it seems to me, is the analytical question that cannot be divorced from the empirical inquiries upon which Professor Ehrlich's study has launched us.

The question concerns not the formality of texts, nor the breadth and vagueness of some norms against the specificity of others, but rather the extent to which they appear to be treated as obligatory in practice. Next to the practice of international officials, I suggest, such evidence of international law in action may best be sought in the positions toward competing claims taken by third parties which have no, or no over-riding, political stake in the immediate controversy. Such a third party may take the view, in or out of an international forum, that its interest in the legal principle involved exceeds its political preference between the contending parties. Or it may view a careful legal stance as its best defence when urged by a powerful party to take an unpalatable position on the merits of the issue. These were, indeed, two functions of the traditional law of neutrality which still serve nations to whom neutrality is an indispensable premiss of foreign policy. As a modest beginning, then, studies of the impact of inter-

Crisis at the United Nations: The Price of Peace Keeping', 33 U.Chi.L.Rev. 249 (1966).

national law on national decisions might widen their perspective from the decisions of the parties primarily engaged to include a look at the view of the law taken by some carefully selected third parties. What position might, say, the Netherlands or Japan take with respect to the liability of the different parties in Cyprus for any injury to a ship, citizen, or property resulting from the various actions described by Ehrlich? To what extent did the diplomatic positions of governments without an ideological pre-commitment toward the Cyprus problem seem to reflect legal premisses? Such evidence, if it can be found, not only shows law as bearing upon the decisions of governments other than the main actors; indirectly it also furnishes the needed evidence of that 'law' whose impact on the main actors is the central focus of these studies.

Finally, of course, we may accept as showing law in action any persuasive evidence that a government concluded, publicly or secretly, in parliamentary debate or in the documents of its executive policy process, that 'such-and-such action would best serve our objectives, but we are bound to a different course by a rule of international law'. Such evidence is rare, and not only because it rarely happens. Proponents genuinely concerned with the legality of a policy will feel a strong urge to argue that what is legal is also pragmatically best, not that a disadvantageous policy is right because it complies with the law.

iv

'Most important,' Professor Ehrlich asks, 'what steps can be taken to improve and strengthen the role of law in ordering relations among nations?' Roger Fisher writes, in the Foreword: 'If we could increase the degree to which the international community is a community under law, the world might be a better place. But how?' In answering these questions, analytical assumptions about 'law' will shape the conclusions that may be drawn from this and similar empirical studies.

If one sees the decisions of national leaders as a function of the national political process, one's target is likely to be the input of legal considerations within the institutions of that process, through strengthened legal offices, parliamentary committees, professional and citizens' associations, and the like. If one sees law as a datum of social psychology and of acculturization, the target will expand to encompass the perceptions and values of the national society, or at least its élites. Conventional positivists may concentrate on the need for more, clearer, and better rules of international law, while others will go further and see the only hope for genuine 'law' in stronger international institutions to administer and 'enforce' those rules. Political decision studies like Ehrlich's tend to see law operate as a prediction of the reactions of other governments in or outside international forums; this focus suggests that governments should be more ready to state and communicate their reactions to one another's contemplated actions with explicit and careful attention to legal premises. Systems analysts add that the premises communicated should be chosen for their systemic implications in an international régime of reciprocity, not just for the immediate situation.[4]

These and other approaches to strengthening the role of law are cumulative, not alternative, and often they describe the same conclusion in different words. Nevertheless, there are pitfalls in an uncritical eclecticism. Strengthening a national society's perception of the sanctity of 'legal rights', for instance, may get in the way when its leaders are prepared to compromise legal claims for a sensible solution, a problem shown here in the formation of British and Turkish policy. More and clearer substantive rules may splinter more often and more clearly under the impact of national infraction, discrediting in the process a more modest potential for international law. Something similar seems to have resulted from writing constitutional guarantees for Turkish Cypriots into the 1960 Accords, assuming Cyprus cannot effectively be held to them. To choose among means of strengthening 'law', one must decide what function of the law is to be strengthened.

It is natural, in an age appalled by the consequences of unconstrained national power in an anarchical world order, to rally around the banner of international law—to reassure ourselves and others that international law exists, that it does affect events, and that it offers hope for the future. Starting with the premiss that international law is a good thing, one tends to welcome evidence that there is more of it around than the sceptics believe. But an undifferentiated enthusiasm for evidence of 'international law' of any kind may get in the way of useful analysis. How helpful, for instance, is it to the analysis of 'law' in international relations to show that governments often refrain from flagrantly aggressive

[4] See note 1, *supra*.

behaviour that may well be within their power? Behaviour that corresponds to an accepted norm is not by itself persuasive evidence of law. The observation that most people support their children or refrain from homicide does not greatly illuminate the role of the laws of child support or of murder. How helpful is the common urge to identify rightness and lawfulness, the urge to find that 'bad' actions are not only undesirable but unlawful, and desirable actions are lawful? Is the role of law served by translating all claims of justice, equity, or ideology into claims of right, or rather by taking seriously the choice of governments sometimes to commit themselves legally and sometimes not, to some parties but not to others? Again, viewing 'law' from the perspective of social psychology and group behaviour one may find virtue in procedural wrangles as a 'cooling-off device'. From this view the role of law might presumably be 'strengthened' in some instances by making available opportunities for bigger and better procedural snarls—an insight worthy of Dickens or Daumier but perhaps not immediately apparent to, say, Ethiopia in the League of Nations.

The answer to the question posed for these studies by Thomas Ehrlich and by Roger Fisher is facilitated if attention is focused first on that part of the spectrum of 'international law' where it operates most as law—in institutional, procedural, and substantive provisions for specific, on-going functions rather than in great principles to govern national policy—not because these roles of law are more important but because they are more law. This is where we find the forms of law performing genuine functions of law as a source of authority and as a constraint on discretion, and where every norm is not paired with a counter-norm. There is more of law in the authority of an agency independent of national parties—a Human Rights Commission, an armistice control commission, a secretary-general, an inspection team— to proceed on its own initiative to investigate, to hear a complaint, to discuss, to confront governments at a minimum with the political costs of nonco-operation, than there is in the most glowing rhetorical standards of right and wrong behaviour between nations. If legal analysis cannot contribute first to the operational role of law in international processes, it can hardly hope to bring 'law' to bear on the substance of the policy issues that endanger the international community.

What is the practical point of such insistence on an analytical differentiation among phenomena that present themselves in the guise of 'law'? It means that the contribution of law as law is to be judged and improved at that end of the spectrum of these phenomena which deals with processes, and with specific substantive solutions, and not weighed or balanced against wider, more general policy goals or values that also appear as norms of 'international law'. From the standpoint of policy, indeed, it may often be necessary to choose between sacrificing the correct application of a rule of the legal process or sacrificing a more important substantive value, and the decision is helped politically by phrasing this greater value as a principle of international law. A decision outside the legal rule may well promote justice, peace, or another good policy. But from the standpoint of the observer interested in the role of law with a view to its improvement, it will prove more productive to see such decisions clearly as choices of policy over law, and to evalute them as such, than to see them as 'strengthening' law.

Of course this conclusion casts doubt on some cherished modes of thought in the American tradition that combines policy premisses with legal realism. Experience and reflection may show that a more modest and rigorous approach to 'law' will be both better realism and better policy. Does it 'strengthen' international law to interpret carefully drafted instruments—treaties, United Nations resolutions, status-of-forces accords—as creating legal 'expectations' beyond their terms, or rather to act on the premiss that the legal relations created by an instrument are those which it was possible to express in its terms?

Ehrlich reports that Cyprus regarded as a major victory, and Turkey as a defeat, the 1965 General Assembly resolution 'calling on' nations to refrain from intervention in Cyprus. No doubt this would be so, and no doubt it might affect the parties' assessments of the position of other governments and thus influence their respective behaviour. Whether this is an instance of the effect of law, however, depends on whether such a General Assembly resolution could, as a matter of law, modify the earlier resolution of the Security Council. Much contemporary literature is devoted to ascribing legal effect to 'recommendations' and to preambulatory paragraphs of Security Council and General Assembly resolutions, apparently in the conviction that this strengthens international law. Why? Does it not leave the political effect of such actions just about as great or as small if they are not 'law'—

and leave the usefulness of the concept of law greater? Did it strengthen the role of international law to force the issue of General Assembly financing of UNEF and ONUC to a questionable decision in the International Court of Justice, or did it weaken it?

Obviously opinions will differ on questions like these. The point of the present comment is not to press one or the other opinion.[5] It is only to suggest that theoretical questions about international law are deeply imbedded in any empirical study of the functioning of law in the crucial context of international security against violence. They must be faced in drawing operative lessons from such empirical studies. With his review of national decisions concerning Cyprus, Professor Ehrlich has given our efforts in this direction an excellent start.

[5] Mine appears in a review of Falk and Mendlovitz, *The Strategy of World Order*, in 19 Stan L. Rev. 1382, 1388 (1967).

INDEX